LAWYERS FOR THE LEFT

IN THE COURTS, IN THE STREETS, AND ON THE AIR

MICHAEL STEVEN SMITH

OR Books
New York · London

All rights information: rights@orbooks.com
Visit our website at www.orbooks.com

First printing 2019

Library of Congress Cataloging-in-Publication Data: A catalog record for this book is available from the Library of Congress.
British Library Cataloging in Publication Data: A catalog record for this book is available from the British Library.

Typeset by Lapiz Digital, Chennai, India. Printed by BookMobile, USA, and CPI, UK.

paperback ISBN 978-1-68219-195-8 • ebook ISBN 978-1-68219-196-5

This book is dedicated to three wonderful people: my late friend Michael Ratner, my nephew Ben Elson, and my son Eli Smith.

CONTENTS

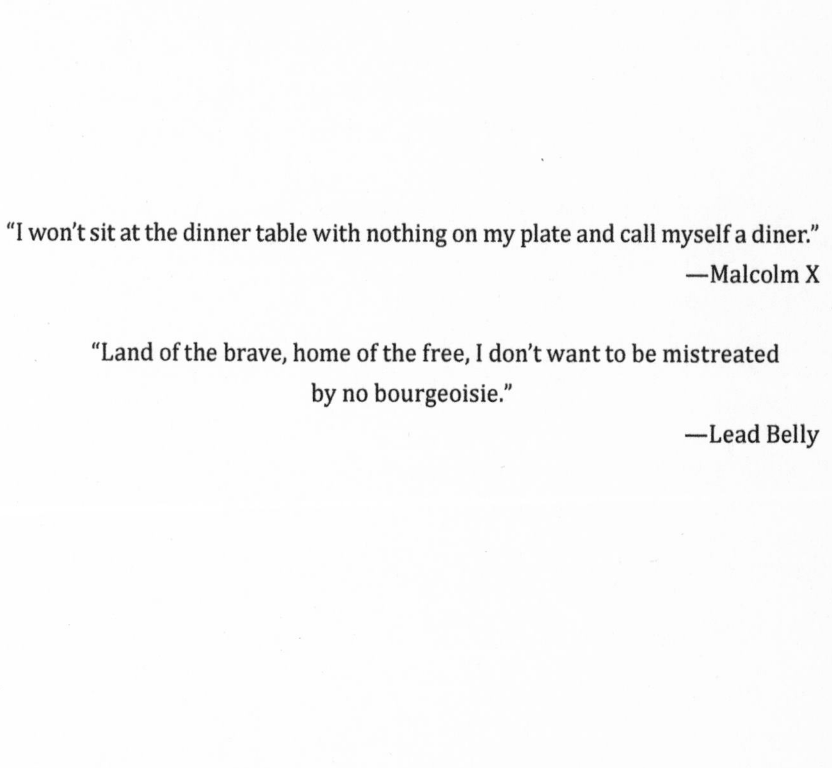

"I won't sit at the dinner table with nothing on my plate and call myself a diner."

—Malcolm X

"Land of the brave, home of the free, I don't want to be mistreated
by no bourgeoisie."

—Lead Belly

FOREWORD

America is in a constitutional crisis. A haughty executive branch flaunts the rule of law. Nine jurists comprise a politicized Supreme Court that churns out cases along party lines. Lawmakers have lost what little backbone they had. Meanwhile, locally, law enforcement officers seem to gun down African American men and boys with complete impunity. It's no wonder that the public has lost faith in the justice system. Our system of checks and balances is in disarray.

Lawyers for the Left is an antidote for those disillusioned by the rule of law's demise. It offers up a series of engaging and intimate profiles in integrity. The stories in these pages will give readers hope: they bring to life a healthy resistance by a special breed of lawyers actively taking on seemingly intractable problems.

Across the United States, thousands of individuals dedicate their lives to advancing issues, causes, and people challenging the status quo. Some survive on pauper wages. Many face daunting opposition—overzealous prosecutors, intractable courts, and a staid legal system in which property interests transcend humanitarian ones. But they persevere. They are lawyers for the left.

They challenge traditional notions of how one must practice law. They are also known as "cause lawyers" or "people's lawyers," because their moral compasses gravitate to issues and people. Rather than practice a kind of conformist lawyering that sees the law as fixed and immovable, they take their cues from communities in need. They ask themselves how the law can be adapted to help to rectify injustice.

These practitioners rarely get credit for helping to shape the legal landscape in our democracy. But they provide a critical check on society's dominant powers. Something in their DNA animates them to challenge privileged viewpoints. And they stand out as champions of the best aspirations within all of us.

Many began by defying the dominant law school curriculum and methods of teaching. American law schools prevent young lawyers from making autonomous decisions about the way they will practice law. Unlike most, these rebellious students refused to adhere to a model espousing ultimately self-serving values. They could not ignore the moral and political content of our laws. The knowledge of human nature, not just the letter of the law, informs the social import of their work.

***

In the 1950s, at the height of anti-communist hysteria, it took courage to stand up to the FBI. But the National Lawyers Guild was unlike any other bar association or legal organization. It refused to ask its members to take loyalty oaths, and proudly stood with radicals fighting racism and economic oppression.

When its members represented targets of the time—Ethel and Julius Rosenberg, the Hollywood Ten, progressive labor leaders, and others—the Lawyers Guild itself became a target of government overreaching. The Department of Justice branded it "subversive." From 1941 on, the FBI deployed over 1,000 informants to report on Guild activities and to disrupt meetings. Agents rummaged through members' trash and tapped telephones. The Bureau falsely maligned the Guild to judges, the public, and the press. After a decade of litigation, the Bureau admitted its charges were baseless.

I began serving as executive director of the Guild two years before the September 11, 2001 attacks. Soon after, Michael Steven Smith invited me to meet Leonard Weinglass, who had gained notice as one of the nation's pre-eminent movement lawyers, representing the likes of SDS leader Tom Hayden of the Chicago Eight and Pentagon Papers whistleblower Daniel Ellsberg. Lenny's then client, former Weather Underground member Kathy Boudin, was up for parole after nearly two decades in prison for taking part in the 1981 Brink's Robbery. Her father, attorney and Guild member Leonard Boudin, had represented the Cuban government and Paul Robeson, among other controversial clients. From atop the World Trade Center, we talked about Kathy's chances, and about Mumia Abu-Jamal, who Len was also defending.

I was thrilled to be in the company of someone I'd looked up to in law school and beyond. The three of us would go on to work on, and advocate for, the case of the so-called Cuban Five. Heroes in Cuba, they were five intelligence officers who infiltrated anti-Castro terrorist groups in Florida, and were arrested and imprisoned for years after they shared their findings with the U.S. government.

In 2004, Michael Steven Smith and Michael Ratner invited me to join them as a co-host of *Law and Disorder Radio*. The show's mission was to highlight how the government was exploiting public fears to install repressive laws that curtailed civil liberties. We could not imagine then that the program would gain increasing relevance after the Bush administration. I took part in several of the interviews included in *Lawyers for the Left* and heard firsthand these remarkable lawyers' stories.

Over the next years, Guild members challenged—with tenacity and creativity—government infringements on civil liberties. After 9/11, Guild lawyers, legal workers, and law students served as legal observers at record numbers of mass assemblies and protests. Guild attorneys tracked down and advocated on behalf of Arab-Americans secretly detained. They fought the use of secret evidence and extraordinary rendition. FBI targets, including environmentalists, animal rights activists, hacktivists, and communities of color, came to rely on Guild legal practitioners after others refused to take their cases. And during the Occupy movement the organization mobilized an unprecedented coast-to-coast defense of arrestees. As a longtime member of this mighty organization, Michael Steven Smith has had unique access to, and forged friendships with, some of the leading lawyers on the left.

To some, these men and women are pariahs. Yet as time passes, their value to society sharpens in focus.

***

This book is a history unlike any other. It brings to life several seminal people's lawyers. Their ways of practicing law have enriched society and leveled the playing field for untold thousands. You will read stories of how several defied authority to reshape the political and legal landscape. Len Weinglass did this. William Kunstler represented Joey Johnson in the Supreme Court's landmark flag-burning case. Mara Verheyden-Hilliard secured policy-changing First Amendment victories in public parks and sidewalks. Agile in the courtroom and the streets, they understood the measuring stick of success: how legal activities affect the morale and understanding of the people involved. They listened and took their cues from their clients. Each time they stepped into a courtroom, they used it to educate the public about a different social injustice.

They challenged the view that the law should be apolitical. They fought both societal and legal mores. In cooperation with community members, legal workers, and law students, they redefined how law should be used—as an instrument for remedying oppressive policies and practices. Importantly, they know that litigation is just one tactic in a broader campaign, so that sometimes the actual winning of a trial is less important than bringing the message to the public fore.

While most lawyers advise their clients not to speak publicly or engage in protest actions pending trial, these lawyers see it as their mission to strengthen, rather than weaken, their case. Many are National Lawyers Guild members. This radical bar association is dedicated to "the need for basic change in the structure of our political and economic system," according to its preamble. A support system of like-minded persons of conscience was important to these advocates whose courageous stances often left them ostracized and at risk.

Radical lawyers enjoyed widespread political support in the 1960s and 1970s as vibrant anti-war and civil rights movements influenced public opinion and brought about several watershed decisions. Support for cause lawyering assumed a different relevance under the Reagan and subsequent administrations, and with the rise of globalization. Social justice movements and organizations came to rely on left lawyers to fill widening service gaps as corporations' power in society grew. At the same time, National Lawyers Guild members and other progressive organizations realized the importance of mentoring new generations of socially-conscious attorneys. They understood their responsibility of mentoring those who would walk the same path they did, and helped encourage and teach aspiring movement law students and lawyers.

With this book, there is hope that more Americans will appreciate the critical role of the brave individuals like those profiled herein. Even better, it should galvanize more law students and young attorneys to follow in the footsteps of these many inspiring lawyers for the left.

Heidi Boghosian, Esq.
Executive Director, National Lawyers Guild (1999-2014)

INTRODUCTION

THE CHALLENGES FACING LAWYERS FOR THE LEFT

On September 11, 2001, I was living with my wife Debby and my talking parrot Charlie Parker one block from the World Trade Center. If the building had fallen over instead of in on itself it would've flattened us. We spent the night in the dark without a phone, electricity, or water.

The next day the police came through the building telling us we had to evacuate. We put Charlie in his traveling cage and started walking through the ash towards Greenwich Village to stay with our friends Michael Ratner and Karen Ranucci. Charlie kept saying to everybody we encountered, "It's OK, It's OK." But it wasn't OK. Not for Charlie, who kept nodding out on his perch, almost died, and ended up at the Animal Medical Center with avian respiratory disease. And not for Debby and me, whose law office was just across the street from the collapsed twin towers. The building was so polluted we couldn't get into it for a year.

Our immediate challenge was to find a new office. Initially we'd thought that our building had been destroyed. After moving up to the Catskill Mountains, we got a call from our son Eli in Ohio, who saw our building on television. Except for a couple of broken windows, the twenty-story office building on the corner of Church and Vesey was still standing. So we borrowed a pushcart from our friend, the human rights lawyer and former U.S. Attorney General Ramsey Clark; secured the help of a police officer stationed on the corner; and, flashlights in hand, climbed up to the fourth floor to retrieve our legal files.

A month later, after our apartment had been decontaminated, we set up shop in our dining room/living room. As we piled up our legal files on a table in one corner and restored Charlie to his cage in another, Debby got a call from a nasty insurance company rep. Our firm represented seriously injured people. We sued insurance companies. Like all major cities and much of the U.S., New York is run by finance, insurance, and real estate corporations—a ruling-class conglomerate known by the acronym FIRE. Charlie, who loves Debby and is very protective of her, overheard the insurance guy abusing Debby. He got more and more agitated, walking back and forth on his perch. Finally, imitating my exact tone of voice, he yelled out, "I'm going to kick your ass, you son-of-a-bitch." But it hasn't worked out that way. We've been the ones getting our asses kicked during the almost two decades since 9/11.

With bipartisan support, President Bush used 9/11 as a rationale to rush the over 300-page Patriot Act through Congress. In the works for three years before 9/11, the Act provided for extensive, increased government surveillance on U.S. citizens. The FBI can now monitor every phone call, e-mail, text and every stroke on a computer or phone—including financial and medical records—all without a court order.

Next, but still within days of the attacks, Bush had Congress approve the Authorization for Use of Military Force. The following month, he issued Military Order Number One. Together, these provisions give unprecedented authority to the president. Michael Ratner, then-head of the Center for Constitutional Rights (CCR), called it a "coup." Bush was now authorized to use military force against nations, organizations, and individuals his administration suspected of "terrorism." And he could capture and detain forever without trial any non-U.S. citizen the administration deemed to be a "terrorist."

The most dramatic demonstration of this radically expanded executive power was the murder by drone—in Yemen, and without due process of law—of Anwar-al-Awlaki, a vocal Muslim cleric and an American citizen. The CCR was retained by al-Awlaki's father, but Anwar's case was thrown out of court because the court said that the father lacked standing to sue on behalf of his son. Al-Awlaki was assassinated, which amounts to a political murder. Several weeks later, al-Awlaki's sixteen-year-old son was also killed.

In 2011, President Obama signed into law the National Defense Authorization Act, a bill drafted in secret, behind closed doors. The Act authorizes the U.S. military to pick up and indefinitely imprison American citizens and civilians in their own backyards without charge or trial, in effect extending the foreign "battlefield" to the entire United States. The provision also effectively legalizes the assassination of American citizens without charge or trial.

President Trump now claims the power to pardon himself. His conservative justices constitute a majority on the Supreme Court, which will likely uphold provisions authorizing unchecked authority for the executive branch. Leftist lawyers and the movements they represent now face all-pervasive governmental spying and the consolidation of the authoritarian state, which has life-and-death powers.

Lamenting the lack of a socialist movement that could defend democracy and the rule of law, the late Belgian socialist Ernest Mandel wrote, "We are at the foot of the Himalayas without adequate tools but we must climb up." Ultimately, the social gains the American people have won since the 1930s are on the chopping block. Working stealthily over the last thirty years, the radical right now holds a majority in thirty-three states, and controls both the Supreme Court and the presidency. Funded by the Koch Brothers and other billionaires and wealthy supporters, the extreme right's goal is to "dismantle the administrative state" and take away every social benefit that political movements have earned since the 1930s. They plan to call a constitutional convention to permanently institute their program. As a model, the right looks to its success in advising Chilean dictator General Augusto Pinochet. To prevent us from fighting back, they have restricted democracy with voter suppression, the gutting of the 1965 Voting Rights Act, and extensive gerrymandering since the 2010 census.

In its Citizens United decision, the Supreme Court has declared that corporations have the same right that people do to free speech—and are allowed to use unlimited funds to influence elections, including from undisclosed, "dark" sources. I will believe that corporations are "people" the day one of them gets a colonoscopy.

The left has recently lost Supreme Court cases on gerrymandering, voter suppression, gay rights, and the Muslim travel ban. Even a woman's right to make decisions about her own body is in danger.

With six corporations owning the major media outlets, the public's access to information has been severely restricted. New algorithms employed by Google and Facebook limit access to people seeking alternative media, such as *Democracy Now!, Black Agenda Report, The Real News Network*, Chris Hedges' *On Contact,* and *Law and Disorder Radio*, the weekly one-hour radio show I co-host with Attorney Heidi Boghosian.

We are on the defensive, and our institutional capacity to hold back the assault is being eroded.

What is law?

Though the challenges leftist lawyers face today are great, they are not unprecedented. And we can learn much from radical lawyers of the past. Martin Luther King's courageous attorney William Kunstler and Federal District Judge Jack Weinstein both received awards from the New York State Association of Criminal Defense Attorneys in 1994. But each had a very different view of the law. In his acceptance speech, Kunstler said that he thought Judge Weinstein believed that law was "that considered response of a civilized society to the problem of reaching a reasoned conclusion to disputes between the state and its citizens and among the latter themselves. Whatever its shortcomings, they are patently aberrational and remediable." Kunstler believed this was the liberals' view of the law.

Kunstler's own view was different. He said that the law "in fundamental essence, is nothing more than a method of control created by a socio-economic system determined, at all costs, to perpetuate itself by all and any means necessary, for as long as possible." When asked about democratic rights, Kunster's friend, the late and deeply respected attorney Leonard Weinglass, said he did not believe, ultimately, that capitalism and democracy were compatible. We are seeing the consequences of this contradiction unfold at an accelerated pace.

Lawyers for the left take an activist and oppositional, albeit auxiliary role. We recognize that great movements of the people "from below" are fundamental to social change. And the need to protect our democratic right to speak out, educate, organize, associate, and demonstrate is more crucial than ever, as the Bill of Rights is increasingly threatened. We use our legal training to carve out a space for, defend the legitimacy of, and give legal expression to the fundamentally political movements for social transformation. On a more mundane level, we provide legal services and hence some possibility of justice to individuals who would otherwise have to suffer.

What can we learn from left lawyers of the '40s and '60s?

Opposition to the rightist insurgency in the U.S. is growing, as is support for socialist organizations and ideas. Recent polls find that nearly half of Americans have a favorable view of socialism. Bernie Sanders would have likely won the presidency had he not been thwarted by Hillary Clinton's pro-corporate forces in the Democratic Party. The election of socialists Kshama Sawant in Seattle and Alexandria Ocasio-Cortez in Queens and the Bronx demonstrate the popularity of socialist proposals for health care, housing, education, employment, and women's, immigrants' and LGBTQ rights. As Glen Ford, the editor of *Black Agenda Report,* has written, "The central reality of late-stage capitalism [is its] inability to offer the people anything but widening wars and deepening austerity." As a consequence, radical consciousness is growing in our country. Socialism is no longer a dirty word.

We know from our experience in the '60s that the government, through the FBI and other intelligence agencies, acts as a secret political police force that will try to destroy any Black, socialist, or radical organization threatening those who benefit from the socio-economic system about which Kunstler spoke. The FBI recently revealed that it was spying on and likely attempting to disrupt and destroy those whom it labeled "Black Identity Extremists," that is, Black people who organized to oppose systematic police abuse in their communities.

In 1971, the Socialist Workers Party (SWP), represented by Leonard Boudin, an attorney profiled below, brought a lawsuit against the government's secret political police, including the FBI and CIA, for the government's massive, systematic violation of its members' constitutional rights. I was a member of that organization and attended much of the trial, reporting on it for several magazines. At stake was nothing less than the right to advocate socialist ideas and put them into practice. The government claimed it had the right to spy on, harass, blacklist, and deport those whose political views it disapproved of, even if those political activities were completely legal and protected by the Constitution and/or the Bill of Rights.

The FBI launched its COINTELPRO (Counter INTELigence PROgram) operation against the SWP in 1961. The Party sued the FBI, enlisted wide support, and after fifteen years of litigation, several appeals and a trial, it accomplished something unprecedented in American history. It won the first citizens' case against FBI spying and disruption. What was the extent of the victory? The FBI's stated aim in the operation was revealed: to "expose, disrupt, and otherwise neutralize the activities" of groups it perceived to be a threat to the established order.

The methods it used to harass and suppress the SWP—which will surely continue to be used against organizations as the struggle heats up—included physical and electronic surveillance, burglaries, poison pen letters, trash covers, mail covers, manipulation of the media, deportation of non-citizens, and surprise "visits" to members' relatives, employers, and landlords. From 1960 to 1976, the FBI paid its informers and agents $1.6 million. Fully 300 informers infiltrated the SWP—a relatively small organization—alone. Altogether 1,300 agents were deployed. The government maintained that even if the socialist group did nothing illegal, the government "has the right to keep itself informed of the activities of groups that openly advocate revolutionary change in the structure and leadership of the government of the United States, even if such advocacy might be within the letter of the law."

The case remains extraordinarily important today. It protects the right to legally advocate socialism as crucial to countering capitalism's threat—both nuclear and ecocidal—to life on the planet. The case affirms that any attempt by the FBI to destroy socialists and their organizations is illegal. Boudin wrote, "This lawsuit represented the first wholesale attack upon the entire hierarchy of so-called intelligence agencies that had attempted to infiltrate and destroy a lawful political party."

Further, "For the first time a court had to really examine the FBI's intrusions into the political system of our nation and, in unmistakable language, has condemned the FBI activity as patently unconstitutional and without statutory authority or regulatory authority. The decision stands as a vindication of the First and Fourth Amendment rights not only of the SWP, but of all political organizations and activists in the country to be free of government spying and harassment."

The Necessity Defense

Len Weinglass, an attorney profiled in this book, was lead defense counsel in a significant case. It involved the CIA and the use of the "necessity defense" by students and their supporters, including '60s radical Abbie Hoffman and Amy Carter, President Jimmy Carter's daughter.

When the CIA tried to recruit members at the rural University of Massachusetts campus, they were foiled by the students who held sit-ins. The protesting students were arrested and tried. Len raised the "necessity defense." It permits the commission of a crime if it is used to stop a larger crime. Len alleged that the CIA was a criminal enterprise. He called ex-CIA agent Ralph McGehee to testify about the CIA's illegal overthrow of the democratically elected governments of Iran (in 1953) and Guatemala (in 1964).

Testifying about his own experiences in Vietnam, McGehee described the Agency's assassination of Vietnamese nationalists and communists in its Phoenix Program in the 1960s. In that operation, 20,000 people were murdered.

The local folk on the jury returned a not-guilty verdict. The potential importance of this tactic was underscored recently when the Supreme Court of the State of Minnesota opined that the necessity defense should be allowed in an upcoming trial of climate activists charged with obstructing a tar sands oil pipeline. At the eve of the trail, Judge Robert Tiffany walked back his initial decision to allow the necessity defense. But then, after the prosecution finished its presentation, Tiffany dismissed the case against the defendants on the grounds that the prosecution could not prove that the defendants did any harm to the pipeline.[1]

With Brett Kavanaugh confirmed as a Supreme Court justice, there will be an un-moderated and unmitigated hard-right majority on the U.S. Supreme Court for decades to come. Predictably, it will further erode the two central pillars of American democracy, the Bill of Rights and the separation of governmental powers, which were intended to ensure that the legislative branch share equal power with the executive branch.

We cannot count on the courts to effectively oppose an authoritarian president's extreme-right agenda to roll back social gains and destroy the democratic right to defend and extend them. Six years ago, the CCR Board discussed how we might advance our clients' interests without having to rely on the courts. In his book, *Success Without Victory,* CCR President Jules Lobel advocated using the courts to expose the government and publicize movement clients' issues, including the illegality of many of America's undeclared wars.

"[T]he law generally is designed to maintain the status quo and maintain state power," writes Lobel, "but it is a tension, particularly in modern

[1] See *Minnesota v. Johnston, Klapstein, and Joldersma* (15-CR-16-413, 15-CR-16-414, and 15-CR-17-25).

capitalism, that power is maintained through the use of laws that can be used by the oppressed to challenge that power. The key task for social movement lawyers is to use the law in a radical way to empower people to help build movements, and to challenge in fundamental ways how state power is used."

Moving Forward

A founder of the Washington, D.C. Partnership for Civil Justice, attorney Mara Verheyden-Hilliard won significant cases against the police there and in New York City. She obtained verdicts that protect masses of people and their right to demonstrate in the streets. "The core of the work we do is that we recognize the underlying social-justice movements and their ultimate goals for human liberation," Verheyden-Hilliard noted on a segment of our radio show, *Law and Disorder*. "When we take on a free-speech case, for example, we're looking not just at a technical violation of the First Amendment—not merely that someone's rights have been violated. As critical as it is to defend the Bill of Rights, there are also larger issues. We want to keep the streets, the sidewalks, and parklands open, because all historical and social change in the United States that has made a difference for people has come from below. It has come from popular movements and popular struggle—not because the politicians decide to give people rights. [It happens] because there is a feeling that the people are demanding [change] and they are going to force it to happen."

The central fact of our political and legal lives is the overwhelming power the corporate capitalist state has accumulated, especially since 9/11. In a previous era, during the time of fascist dictatorships, Antonio Gramsci wrote from his Italian prison cell that we need "Pessimism of the intellect, but optimism of the heart." My friend Peter Weiss, a former vice-president of the Center for Constitutional Rights, now in his nineties, added to Gramsci's resolve:

Denial is not an option,
Despair is not an option,
Resistance is the only option.

"You have to have hope," Ramsey Clark, also in his nineties, told me. "Otherwise you don't do anything."

The attorneys whose lives and achievements are celebrated in this book have worked all their professional lives for the expansion of human rights as opposed to property rights. In so doing, they have worked for true democracy and the rule of law.

But for me and many radical lawyers, there is another crucial step. Capitalism ultimately and increasingly is not compatible with democracy and the rule of law. Marx studied law. Both Castro and Lenin were lawyers. For them and for me, there's one way out of the impending catastrophe—the ongoing ecocide, the heightened threat of nuclear annihilation, the crushing of democracy. And that is the building of a mass movement that will take political power to replace our current system with a genuine economic and political democracy. Imagine living in a socialist USA.

***

This book is a compilation of profiles and interviews of radical lawyers. Most are from the '60s—my generation.

As Lewis Lapham has observed, "A person denied knowledge of its past cannot make sense of its present or imagine its future."

These are lawyers and activists that in one way or another participated in the essential struggles of their own times. They could "sense the future in the instant," as Shakespeare said. And they understood that those who are above the struggle are also beside the point.

I have not imposed any formal uniformity on the material presented here. In some instances the biographical account is more full than others. Nor is the length of any one chapter an indication of the relative importance of the lawyer or activist.

To those lawyers and activists who are themselves deeply immersed in the political life of our stirring and difficult age, I hope this book will introduce new allies and fresh sources of strength.

HOW I FOUND THE NATIONAL LAWYERS GUILD

The National Lawyers Guild in the early '60s was not so easy to find, especially if you were from Wisconsin. The culture of the witch hunt still prevailed. I had come east to New York and was at New York University Law School in 1964, where I was one of two radicals in the freshman class. The other had been a founder of Students for a Democratic Society at Ann Arbor.

The Guild in the early '60s was bowed, but unbroken. It fought successfully to not be placed on the attorney general's list of subversive organizations. It had a chapter in New York City, but zero presence at NYU as far as we knew. It took my transferring out of NYU to the law school at the University of Wisconsin to make the connection. It was fortuitous, as I suspect most additions to the NLG's ranks were in those days before the broad student radicalization, which was to come around 1968, four years later.

NYU Law cost $5,300 a year and I ran out of money, or more precisely, my parents and I ran out of money. They had two other children in college at the time. I had grown up in Fox Point, a small Republican village north of Milwaukee, and had set my hopes on escaping. I went to the University of Wisconsin as an undergrad and now found myself disappointedly back there, this time in their law school, which charged $100 a semester in tuition. I was able to work for my room and board.

But Wisconsin had a deservedly progressive reputation and it was there at the law school that I met Karen Mills, who would be my connection to the Guild. She was a red-diaper baby from Great Neck, via Brooklyn Heights. Her dad, Saul Mills, was a historical figure, I later learned. He had been a reporter for the *Brooklyn Eagle* and an organizer of the Newspaper Guild before becoming secretary to John L. Lewis, the head of the militant United Mine Workers and the newly formed CIO.

Saul Mills needed legal help, and he got it from two young lawyers with whom he would become friends and who had recently started up a new firm. They were Leonard Boudin and Victor Rabinowitz. The firm, Rabinowitz, Boudin, and Standard, would become the great fighting leftist firm for the next generation.

Meanwhile, my new friend Karen was friends with Joannie Rabinowitz, Victor's daughter. They had gone to Antioch College, another progressive place, and Joannie came out to Madison to visit. That summer I was to be a clerk in a firm in Oakland, California. Joannie was heading west too and told me she would be organizing farm workers with Cesar Chavez in the Salinas Valley. (Three years before she had organized for civil rights down south. While marching in an integrated demonstration some Ku Kluxer type on the sidelines yelled out to her, "You New York commie Jew nigger lover," to which she shouted back, simply and proudly, "You're right.")

Joannie took me over to have Sunday supper with a woman who was a friend of her family's. That's how I got to meet the extraordinary Ann Fagan Ginger. Ann was welcoming and talkative. She lived in a modest Bay Area house with a detached garage. If this government did things right that garage today would be a national monument, for it housed the Alexander Meiklejohn Library. It was a tremendous resource for lawyers litigating civil rights cases.

Ann showed me the library and told me about the Guild. I liked what I saw and heard, although I was a little uneasy, knowing that by associating with people of her political coloration I was crossing a line that I suspected the government would know about. But in the end, I figured, so what.

I finished law school a year later and to escape the draft joined VISTA, a sort of domestic Peace Corps, and moved to Detroit to do poverty law and tenant organizing in the inner city. There I met the Guild on the battle lines. Jim

Lafferty was there, having just finished being national secretary and running for Congress against the Vietnam War. Future Guild president Bill Goodman was there in the firm started by his father Ernie, the first integrated law firm in the country. It was called Goodman, Crockett, Eden, Robb, and Bedrosian. It came out of the rise of the United Automobile Workers, the great CIO union, and went on to spearhead the Guild's civil rights work in the South in the early '60s.

A year after I got there, future Guild leaders Dick Soble and Buck Davis reported for duty at VISTA. In 1969 we formed an NLG firm called Lafferty, Reosti, Papahkian, James, Stickgold, Smith, and Soble. We had a non-lawyer woman, Linda Mass, as a partner, but couldn't list her on the letterhead. In an interoffice memorandum on December 1, 1970, Lt. Dennis Mulaney, Detroit Police Department Red Squad, wrote, "There is hardly an underground newspaper, liberation, or left-wing group of any kind in Detroit that at one time or another was not represented by the law firm . . ."

We have all been Guild supporters and activists through the years. But it was my singular good fortune to meet Joannie Rabinowitz and to go over to Ann Ginger's home for dinner forty-two years ago.

Originally published in slightly different form as "1965: How I First Found the National Lawyers Guild," Michael Steven Smith's Notebook, *May 29, 2007.*

MY DETROIT YEARS

I came to Detroit with a draft deferment in September 1967 after graduating from the University of Wisconsin Law School. I chose Detroit via VISTA, rather than the infantry in Vietnam. VISTA gave me the choice of Chicago or Detroit, and I thought that you could do more politically in Detroit.

I found myself a little apartment for fifty bucks a month on Willis Avenue. Formerly, it had been a whorehouse. It was across the street from the Willis Showbar, a topless joint. I could glance out the window and see a neon sign blinking on and off twenty-four hours a day: "Welcome Delegates, Welcome Delegates."

I was assigned to Community Legal Services, a part of the War on Poverty. There were ten would-be lawyers. All of us had graduated from law school and had passed the bar, but none of us knew what we were doing. The program was headed up by Warfield Moore, an attorney who's now a judge in Detroit.

We were supposed to represent community organizations. If they needed a lawyer we were there to service them. I was there with a lot of time on my hands. I read all three volumes of Trotsky's *History of the Russian Revolution* and I really got to understand the revolutionary dynamics of the national question. I read much of Lenin. I also read Earl Ofari's *The Myth of Capitalism,* which is what Nixon was later to advocate.

Along with Ron Reosti, who became the head of Community Legal Services after Warfield left, I represented a guy named Fred Lyles, who formed the United Tenants Union with headquarters on Grand River near Twelfth Street.

The first time we met Lyles he was lying sick in bed. The incinerator in his building was spewing up smoke that went into his room. The walls of his room were gray from this stuff. You could imagine what his lungs looked like.

We went from his individual problem to the building's problem to organizing a whole number of buildings. Lyles became the president of the organization, and we were his lawyers. We got to the point where we had a number of buildings on rent strike. When the landlords would move to evict the tenants, Reosti would have the tenants call up the city enforcement arm. When the landlords moved to evict them for nonpayment of rent, our defense was, it's a retaliatory eviction based on our exercising our constitutional rights to complain to a governmental agency about an illegality. We'd get a stay on an eviction until the place was straightened up. Well, the landlords didn't want to spend money fixing up the buildings.

We wound up engineering the purchase of thirteen buildings, owned and run by the tenants themselves. The thing that forced the owner to sell was that we told him that we were going to take a couple of busloads of his tenants out to his country club. Next week we met with him in his office. This guy was a wonderful creep. He had a beautiful walnut-paneled office with floor-to-ceiling bookshelves. Not only was this guy an entrepreneur and real estate man, he was an intellectual. We learned later that a decorator bought his books by the pound.

The tragic note on all this was that soon after the sale, Lyles was up in his office one night standing in front of a window. A car cruised by and a rifle came out of a window and somebody shot him through the neck. It severed his spinal cord and he became a quadriplegic. The last time I saw him before I left Detroit, he was in a hospital bed, totally paralyzed.

In early 1969, I got elected as chair of the Detroit Committee to End the War in Vietnam, and served a very short stint before I was asked to go down to Columbia, South Carolina, to be the assistant of Leonard Boudin, who was at that time, and for the next twenty years, the great constitutional lawyer in the country. He was chief counsel for GIs United Against the War at Fort Jackson,

South Carolina, a group of and Puerto Rican GIs with one white guy. They had organized a huge anti-war group on the base. These guys were being trained to go to Vietnam. The group was organized against racism in the army, and for the right to communicate their opinions on the war in Vietnam to their elected representatives. They were circulating a petition around the base. The night they got arrested they had called an anti-war rally between two barracks, and two hundred fifty men in uniform attended. The Pentagon went crazy and put nine leaders into the stockade. I went there to help represent these men. We won the case.

Later in Detroit I went to work for Neighborhood Legal Services (NLS), part of the poverty program, with offices on Grand River. We had an experimental law office that was paid for by the government. We were a think tank and could do what we wanted. I remember my first assignment. Arthur Kinoy and Morton Stavis, who are very fine constitutional lawyers, had a firm out east. They had sued the police department in Newark, which had savagely put down the Newark rebellion. They had argued that the police department was politically and morally bankrupt and should be put in receivership. I was sent by NLS to Newark to interview Morton Stavis to find out how they did it, because we were going to sue the Detroit police department to put them in receivership. There was a real wave of police brutality.

When Nixon was elected, all of us at NLS saw the handwriting on the wall. We knew he was going to clip the wings of NLS or try to destroy it. In fact, Nixon, and later Reagan, pretty much crippled it. We bought an old house in the New Center area, just behind the GM building, and fixed it up. Lafferty was good at carpentry. We established the law firm of Lafferty, Reosti, Papakian, James, Stickgold, Smith, and Sobel. Linda Nordquist wasn't a lawyer, but she functioned in every respect as a partner.

We represented just about every movement group in the city. A lot of what we did related to the war in Vietnam. Lafferty became one of the experts in America on draft law. He was published in a book and taught the subject at the University of Michigan. Mark Stickgold did draft law. Dennis James was a wonderful draft-law counselor. We became famous. There were articles about us in *Time* and various newspapers. Before we knew it, we had more clients than we knew what to do with. Nobody else did draft work. We represented Freddy Perlman, an anarchist, and we donated the money for him to buy his first printing press. We were totally nonsectarian.

And we made a living at it. I think we grossed $250,000 our first year, a lot of money then, a lot of money now, because of our draft work. I remember somebody came to us from Grosse Pointe whose father was an arms manufacturer. Dennis James reported at our partnership meeting on Friday that this guy was our client and we were going to charge him so much. We thought about it for a second and we said, "No, let's charge him twice as much." The father called up and yowled about it, and we said he could go somewhere else if he liked. We got the money. Then we turned around and financed a lot of the movement with the money we made. We never thought about making money. We were interested in building the movement.

An insurance agent came over to sell us life insurance. We put Mark Stickgold on him. Stickgold never wore a suit. I used to tell Mark, "You know, you can't get a decent fee unless you look like you're worth it." But Mark didn't abide by that. He was very open and casual with his clients. The life insurance agent came in with his attaché case up to Mark's third-floor office, and Mark met him in his blue jeans. I was in the office next door, so I could hear the conversation. The guy gave Mark the pitch for the insurance. Mark listened to him and then said, "You know, the reason we're not going to take the life insurance is because we think there's going to be a revolution in this country and it's going to take care of widows and orphans and elderly people and anybody who would otherwise need life insurance." I saw the guy walk out of our door shaking his head like he couldn't believe it. But that was our attitude.

I joined the Socialist Workers Party (SWP) in 1968. The SWP had been in Detroit since the '30s. Its origins were in the left wing of the Socialist Party under Debs and in the International Workers of the World (IWW). I had been influenced by the IWW and their notion of industrial democracy and their free speech fights.

I knew I was a Socialist. I didn't think that what existed in the Soviet Union was Socialism. I knew they had replaced capitalism, but they didn't have the kind of democratic rights and humanistic society that I was for. So I didn't support the regime in the Soviet Union, although I was very much influenced by and supportive of the Cuban revolution. I was attracted by the SWP because it had opposed the degeneration of the revolution in Russia. The SWP was very active in the anti-war movement, which was where my heart was ever since law school.

There were about twenty-five members when I joined. They had the Friday Night Militant Labor Forum, a real institution in Detroit, where they invited people of different political persuasions to speak and engage in discussion. I got quite an education from them. The forum started in 1954, when the Communist Party was disintegrating, when there was an attempt made to pull things together in an open forum. It was a good idea then; it's a good idea now.

The other thing that was very important to me was nationalism. SWP had been an early supporter of Malcolm X. George Breitman, who had lived in Detroit until 1967, had edited *Malcolm X Speaks* and had written the book *Malcolm X: The Evolution of a Revolutionary.* I had read his works. I had heard Malcolm speak in Wisconsin and was very shaken up when he was murdered. In Detroit, you could really see nationalists. There was this feeling of dignity and energy that I had never experienced before.

The SWP degenerated after a time, I think mainly because the political situation in America was just so adverse to any left-wing organization. It affected all of us. We were all in the same boat, but in different seats. The SWP turned inward and became very sectarian and expelled a lot of its people, including me. I was the first one kicked out in New York because I disagreed with what they were doing and I didn't keep my mouth shut.

It's always important for Socialists to be up front in what they think, in what they say, and in their vision of what a future society would be like. And it shouldn't be in utopian terms. I also think it's important for us to treat each other decently as comrades.

I stayed in Detroit from 1967 to 1971. Those were very good years. If there was one lesson I learned from being in Detroit, it was seeing how people could come together and make a difference.

Originally published as part of "The Changing Visions of Detroit's Male Left," in Robert H. Mast, Detroit Lives *(Philadelphia: Temple University Press, 1994), 296–300.*

WHEN RADICAL LAWYERS TAKE TO THE AIRWAVES: AN INTERVIEW BY *THE INDYPENDENT*

INDYPENDENT: How did you meet your two co-hosts, Michael Ratner and Heidi Boghosian?

MICHAEL STEVEN SMITH: Michael Ratner lived around the corner from me in the Village. This is twenty-five years ago. He was elected as president of the National Lawyers Guild and came over to ask me to work on their magazine, *Guild Notes*. We've been friends and comrades ever since. Heidi was hired as executive director of the Guild a dozen years ago. We started doing "Free Mumia" work together.

INDYPENDENT: Are the three of you practicing law?

SMITH: When I got out of law school I thought, well, I wasn't going to practice law just to make rich people richer. Michael and Heidi thought the same. I dodged the Vietnam draft by getting into the domestic version of the Peace Corps. They sent me to Detroit's inner city to do poverty law. I did tenant organizing and was active in the anti-war movement and I got the book *Malcolm X Speaks* into the city's bookstores. When I left the program, I was too old to be drafted and I helped start up a movement law firm.

INDYPENDENT: What kind of work did you do?

SMITH: We advised DRUM, the Dodge Revolutionary Union Movement, which was a radical organization of autoworkers in Detroit. And we represented people resisting the draft and organizing against the war in the military. I went down to Fort Jackson, South Carolina, on a case called The Fort

Jackson 8. The extraordinary Leonard Boudin was the main lawyer. We won and extended First Amendment rights for soldiers to march in protests and to publish anti-war newspapers and keep them in their lockers. When the GIs started turning against the war, it was all over. Then I moved to New York City in 1971, worked for Pathfinder Press, a Socialist publishing house, and got a job at Harlem Legal Services. From there, I moved on to represent indigent merchant seamen at The Center for Seafarers' Rights. I ran their legal aid program. Lately I have been suing insurance companies on behalf of injured persons.

INDYPENDENT: What about Michael and Heidi?

SMITH: Michael clerked for federal judge Constance Baker Motley when he got out of law school, practiced criminal law briefly, and then joined the staff at the Center for Constitutional Rights, which came out of the civil rights movement of the '60s. The day after he took the job they sent him up to Attica to deal with the prison rebellion. Bill Kunstler, a founder of the CCR, was already up there. Michael became litigation director and then president. He did a lot of work representing Cuba and the Sandinista revolutionaries in Nicaragua. Now he is representing Julian Assange and WikiLeaks. Hard to believe, but he has been at the CCR for forty years. He is now president emeritus.

Heidi graduated law school at Temple in Philadelphia before heading up the Guild. She is admitted to the bar here and works not just as an organizer but as an author. She has done great work around the country on police abuse and governmental and corporate intrusion on privacy. Her recent book, *Spying on Democracy*, will be the classic on how this government has turned democracy on its head. She has a great radio voice and TV presence and is becoming a spokeswoman for the movement in this regard in national media.

INDYPENDENT: Why and when did you start the show and where did you get the idea?

SMITH: Bush had been elected back in 2000. It was evident that he was morally and intellectually challenged, but it was deeper than that, it was systemic. When Bush and Cheney and the "oil junta" gave the order to attack Iraq, the ultimate crime of aggressive war, on the lie that Saddam Hussein was connected to Al-Qaida, we started thinking about approaching WBAI with the idea for a show on law and public policy. Jim Lafferty, head of the Los Angeles NLG, was an inspiration at Pacifica station KPFK with his popular drive time show. I gave a presentation to the WBAI Program Committee. The program director then was Bernard White. He backed us and we were put on the air every other week. After a time it was every week. Now thanks to WBAI we are on sixty-five stations around the country, from Moscow, Idaho, to two new Pacifica stations in Houston and Washington, D.C. And we get thousands and thousands of Internet hits weekly from around the world. We have a map of this. It is amazing. New Zealand, Russia, Argentina, everywhere.

INDYPENDENT: How did you choose the name *Law and Disorder*?

SMITH: It is the title of a column in a local Kingston, New York, newspaper that chronicles things like DWIs and drugstore break-ins. We thought it was apt for the grander criminals on the national stage.

INDYPENDENT: Looking back over the past decade, what do you think are some of the highlights of the show?

SMITH: We've had great people on from A to Z, from Tariq Ali to the late Howard Zinn. OR Books has asked us to transcribe the most important interviews for a book to come out at the end of this year. Colin Robinson, the partner at OR, says *Law and Disorder* is an intellectual and political history of the last decade and deserves to be gotten out to the movement in book form. One segment that we occasionally run is called "Lawyers You'll Like." We've had great movement lawyers on: Mel Wulf, the former head litigator of the ACLU; Bill Schaap, who did so much to expose CIA crimes; the late Len Weinglass, one of the best constitutional law movement defense lawyers of recent times; Holly Maguigan, who taught at NYU School of Law and is the former co-president of The Society of American Law Teachers, who was recently given the great teacher award; and Ramsey Clark, the former attorney general.

INDYPENDENT: What are your plans?

SMITH: The rule of law has gone to hell in a hand basket. Even former President Jimmy Carter recently said we are no longer living in a democracy.

We expose this, rally people against it. But more broadly speaking we don't think that democracy is compatible with capitalism. Dictatorship is. But not democracy.

I co-edited with Debby Smith and Frances Goldin the visionary book HarperCollins just published called *Imagine: Living in a Socialist USA*. Frances came to us and said she wanted to do two things before she died. She is eighty-nine years old. She said she wanted to free Mumia and to do a book on what America might be like if we got rid of capitalism. Four of the articles in the book are on law.

Michael Ratner wrote one called "What I Would Do If I Were Attorney General." It starts off saying, "It'll be a cold day in hell if someone with my politics was made attorney general." But it is possible if the radicalization, which is just beginning, picks up speed, a lot of it. I wrote the one on civil law. Mumia Abu-Jamal and Angela Davis wrote one on criminal law, and Ajamu Baraka, who is on the Center for Constitutional Rights board with Michael Ratner and me, wrote one on Socialism being the ultimate expression of democracy, both political and economic. The book starts with an indictment of capitalism, has twenty chapters by various authors on how everything—ecology, housing, food, medical care, education, sexuality, science, art, media—would be different if we had a new economic system. The last part is how to get from here to there, from where we are to where we want to be. All the profits from the book are going to the Mumia defense.

INDYPENDENT: How is the book being received?

SMITH: It is amazing. Alice Walker wrote saying, "This is the book we've all been waiting for." It is appealing now because of the dead-end crisis this society is in. Even the establishment *Kirkus Reviews* really liked it and wrote this about one of the contributions to the last segment on how to make the third American revolution: "Historian Paul Le Blanc argues persuasively for a third American revolution mounted by a broad left-wing coalition that could spark a mass Socialist movement" and that "Socialism involves people taking control of their own lives, shaping their own futures, and together controlling the resources that make such freedom possible . . . Socialism will come to nothing if it is not a movement of the great majority in the interests of the great majority . . . People can only become truly free through their own efforts."

INDYPENDENT: Your final thoughts?

SMITH: What Paul wrote is a profound truth. And only with an independent media can we continue our work because only a politically aware, socially committed populace can affect important and lasting change.

MICHAEL RATNER (1943–2016)

There's not a joy the world can give like that it takes away.

—Byron

One of the last times I saw Michael was via FaceTime. He was out of the hospital once again and back in the living room of his Greenwich Village home. I was on the Upper West Side at our singing class with Michael's son, Jake, his companion, Elena, his daughter, Ana, our friend Jenn, and my wife, Debby. We all took a class together called "Anyone Can Sing" from our singing teacher, Elissa. We connected with Michael over an iPhone and sang him "The Internationale," his favorite song. We could see Michael lying back in his lounger. We sang the first verse:

Arise ye prisoners of starvation.
Arise ye wretched of the earth,
For justice thunders condemnation,
A better world's in birth.

He could see and hear us and we could see him. So we sang the second verse.

No more tradition's chains shall bind us,
Arise ye slaves no more in thrall,
The earth shall rise on new foundations,
We have been naught, we shall be all.

Michael knew the history of this anthem of the international working class. Perhaps, as he listened to our passionate rendition, he was recalling that Eugene Poitier wrote the words even as the Paris Commune was being crushed, gun smoke in the air, its leaders lined against the wall at Père Lachaise cemetery in Paris and executed. The Commune endured for ninety-one days. It was the first Socialist uprising of modern times. This was the rebel tradition with which Michael Ratner identified.

We arrived at the last verse:

'Tis the final conflict,
Let each stand in their place,
International solidarity,
Shall be the human race.

Michael teared up and joined in the singing with us—him in the original French. From his chair he raised his right fist in the air, sharing that moment with his children and friends.

Michael believed in democracy and the rule of law. He did not believe they were compatible with capitalism. He knew fascism was.

Michael had initially viewed law as a civilized method of resolving disputes. Whatever flaws it had could be fixed. But he soon came to understand that law was a method of social control by the powers that be who were determined to perpetuate themselves by any means necessary.

It was their government which Michael fought, in court, in the media, in books, and in the classroom, striving tirelessly to expose its lies, its cruelty, its racism, and its imperial reach.

"Law is villainess," he wrote. "Social equality will never be achieved under capitalism."

Harry Ratner, Michael's father, came to Cleveland from anti-Semitic Poland and soon became, along with his brothers, quite successful in business. He married Ann Spott, an intelligent and lovely woman. In the Jewish tradition the highest form of charity is anonymous; Harry Ratner and Ann were extremely charitable. Michael inherited that gene, as did his siblings, Bruce and Ellen. When asked one time whom he helped out, Michael answered, "anyone who asks me." Michael was a non-religious Jew, but rejected Jewish nationalism and embraced instead an unconditional solidarity with the persecuted and exterminated.

Michael will be remembered as a generous, loyal friend and a gentle and kind person. Politically, he was a compelling speaker, an acute analyst of the political scene, and a far-sighted visionary. Professionally, Michael Ratner will live on as one of the great advocates for justice of his time, taking his place in the twentieth century legal pantheon alongside Leonard Boudin, Arthur Kinoy, Morton Stavis, Ernest Goodman, William Kunstler, and Leonard Weinglass.

Michael died in the hospital on a spring afternoon in May. He had hoped to go up to his place in the Catskill Mountains. He would have gone fly-fishing for trout in one of the little streams up there while Karen put in a large vegetable garden and hunted for mushrooms in the woods. He would've gone jogging or biking, or sat in his screened-in living room looking out at the yard full of chickens and Guinea hens and a black-and-white lamb born unexpectedly that spring. Later, he would have joined his family and friends at a large round table where we all frequently met for dinner. But this was not to be.

Michael and Karen created and formed the center of a large movement community, a community that will carry on Michael's work and memory. That is his legacy.

THE FOUNDING GENERATION: LAWYERS YOU'LL LIKE

I am a '60s radical, having graduated from the University of Wisconsin law school in 1967. Radical lawyers in the generation that preceded mine became active in the 1930s in the areas of labor organization, civil rights, and civil liberties.

I write about Victor Rabinowitz, Leonard Boudin, William Kunstler, Conrad Lynn, Ramsey Clark, and Bruce Wright, who were all of the World War II generation: Wright and Clark in Europe, Kunstler in the Pacific.

They were of my parents' generation and all historical figures.

My generation of the 1960s was active in anti-draft and military law, poverty law, homosexual rights, prisoners' rights, women's rights, civil rights, and constitutional litigation.

This book contains essays that remind us of the history of struggle in this country and the role lawyers played in the fight for social justice. These lawyers were involved in the most important cases and struggles of the twentieth century.

Their work began in the labor struggles of the '30s and '40s. In the '50s they defended those attacked by McCarthy and then went south in the early days of the civil rights movement. They were very good at what they did. They understood that the courtroom was a political forum, that cases were won not just in the courts but in the streets.

The legal institutions the WWII generation founded—the National Lawyers Guild, the National Conference of Lawyers, and the Center for Constitutional Rights—represented the best that is America.

These lawyers kept alive the dream of a more just society and passed the torch to the generation of the '60s who advocated for the fight for rights of the poor, LGBTQ, Hispanics, women, immigrants, and anti-war protesters.

WILLIAM KUNSTLER (1919–1995)

A month before he died, Bill Kunstler performed a stand-up routine at Caroline's Comedy Club in Manhattan. I wasn't surprised to see the announcement in the *New York Times*. Bill was entertaining and extremely funny. Recently, he had cracked up a bunch of us outside my office door with a terrific Groucho Marx imitation. His high spirits and irreverence, even about himself, rubbed off on people, making them feel good about themselves. Even though he was seventy-six, he said he would never retire. Instead, he envisioned himself "checking out" while delivering a summation to a jury, sinking to the courtroom floor, clutching his notes. The tagline was that then his partner, Ron Kuby, would grab the notes from his hands and rise to finish the summation.

One of Bill's favorite stories came out of the Chicago Seven trial. Someone had mailed him a vegetable substance, and he immediately called its receipt to the attention of Judge Julius Hoffman. "What are you telling me for?" remarked the obtuse judge (whom the defendants referred to as Mr. Magoo). "Do something with it yourself."

"I assure you, your honor, that I will personally burn it tonight," responded Bill.

I remember when Bill gave a talk on the death penalty at the New York Marxist School a couple of years ago. As he was leaving, a group of people gathered around him asking for his address. "Here is a get-out-of-jail-free card," he offered, producing several business cards from his wallet and handing them out.

I met Bill for the first time in 1966, when I was a law student at the University of Wisconsin. Although he was a generation older than I, we were radicalized at the same time. Truly hundreds of lawyers like myself, products of the '60s, many in the National Lawyers Guild, strongly identified with and were constantly inspired by Bill. He spoke at the law school about government repression, using the metaphor "silken threads" descending and strangling. The honorarium was $1,000, which I was happy to help get for him, and which went from his hands directly into the movement, as usual. I saw him some years later at the City Hall subway entrance. His hand came up from his pocket empty after fishing for a token. "Here," I said, offering him a token and putting it in the slot. "Now it is $1,001," he replied, walking through the turnstile.

Several months ago, Bill was at my office for a deposition. This time, he was the defendant. Michael O'Neill of Syracuse and I had the good fortune of defending him against a trumped-up legal malpractice action. Bill charmed the socks off the opposing attorney, a guy who had flown up with his associate from Washington, D.C., and who had paid a whole lot of money to have Bill's testimony videotaped.

The deposition, with Bill sitting at the end of the table on camera, lasted all day. The D.C. lawyer did not lay a glove on Bill, who remembered in detail events of eight years past. Then, the damnedest thing happened. When Bill got through cleaning the fellow's clock and the deposition ended, the D.C. guy—who had told us during the course of the hearing that he had earlier worked for the Federal Bureau of Prisons as the assistant to the director—got up from the conference table, leaned over, and hugged Bill. And you know, despite Bill's feelings about the Bureau of Prisons, he bore the D.C. guy no personal malice. He hugged him back. Indeed, during the course of the entire morning and afternoon of the deposition, when Bill was being sued for a telephone number that, if enforced, would have wiped him out, Bill had nothing but kind words to say about the plaintiff, and he sincerely meant it.

Incidentally, Bill had lost a letter he had written to the plaintiff. Had Bill been able to produce the letter, the plaintiff's bogus suit would have been shown to be groundless. But he could not find it. "Just say what you had written in it," I volunteered, figuring that any stick would do to beat a dog. But Bill would not do it, and then, as if to show that virtue is sometimes more than its own reward, several weeks later Bill actually found the exculpatory letter.

Bill's seventy-fifth birthday party at Gus's Place, his favorite Village restaurant, was so full of laughs that I was left reeling. He talked about his early childhood in Harlem and told of being a mischievous troublemaker, a "real pisser, Peck's bad boy," as he put it. Truly, as Milton wrote, "Childhood shows the man, as morning shows the day."

Bill went on to relate a story about himself. He had been representing the mobster John Gotti (on the issue of whether Gotti had the right to choose his own lawyer), and he was invited out to dinner with Gotti and his crowd. Bill was asked at the restaurant if he would please make a toast. He rose from the table, glass in hand, and declared, "Here's to crime." The entire gathering sat stone silent staring at him. Bill then exited. After he left, they all fell out.

Bill first got involved in the civil rights movement by representing freedom riders from the North who helped desegregate interstate travel. He stayed committed to the Black struggle for four decades until the end of his life, representing Martin Luther King Jr. as his personal attorney for six years, and recently successfully representing Malcolm X's daughter. He had left a successful Westchester practice with his late brother, Michael, and eventually set up an office in the basement of his house in the Village, which he told me had been a stop on the Underground Railroad.

With characteristic courage, Bill recently confronted a Supreme Court judge, saying he was "a disgrace to the bench" over a racist ruling he had made. The judge then lodged a formal complaint against Bill with the Character and Fitness Committee of the Bar, asking that Bill be "disciplined." Bill found himself in the courthouse downtown in Manhattan. The room was packed with his supporters. Bill spoke about his beliefs and his life: DeWitt Clinton High School, Yale, Phi Beta Kappa, Army major, Second World War in the Pacific, Bronze Star, Columbia Law School (Stone Scholar).

Morton Stavis, Bill's good friend and president of the Center for Constitutional Rights (Bill was a vice president, founder, and volunteer attorney), elicited more of the details on Bill's accomplishments. Then Bill concluded with speaking about his representation of the Attica brothers, Fred Hampton, Assata Shakur, the Harlem Six, and Larry Davis. He spoke of his friendship with Malcolm X, whom he admired immensely. The effect of Bill's testimony on me and everyone else in that room was immense and deeply moving. "We are in the presence of a great and fine American," I thought at the time. The panel must have also had good thoughts, because when their "disciplinary" decision came down, it hardly amounted to a slap on the wrist.

Bill Kunstler's legal accomplishments in the defense of African Americans and democratic rights are of great historical significance. Bill undertook cases, as he would say, to make a point and educate people. Fees were not important to him. Often, he did not charge any fee at all, and when he did, he never kept very good track of it. On wealth, he said, "Just get enough to live on. Animals that overeat die." On his career of litigating, he said in a 1993 interview, "Overall, I never counted, but my lifetime batting average is probably better than Willie Mays's." His victories included:

- Trial Counsel, *Adam Clayton Powell v. McCormack* (1966 reinstatement to Congress case)
- Trial Counsel, *Hobson v. Hansen* (1966 Washington, D.C., school desegregation case)
- Trial Counsel, *Stokely Carmichael v. Allen* (1967 invalidation of Georgia Insurrection Statute)
- Trial Counsel, *Hobson v. Hansen*
- Trial Counsel, *McSurley v. Ratcliff* (1967 invalidation of Kentucky Sedition Statute)
- Trial Counsel, *U.S. v. Berrigan* (1968 defense of Catholic anti-war activists accused of destroying draft records at Catonsville, Maryland)
- Trial Counsel, *U.S. v. Dellinger* (1969–70 Chicago 8 conspiracy case)

- Trial Counsel, *U.S. v. Dennis Banks and Russell Means* (defense of American Indian movement leaders accused of a number of crimes in the takeover of Wounded Knee, South Dakota, in 1973)
- Trial Counsel, *U.S. v. Sinclair* (1971 invalidation of government's claim of unrestricted wiretapping powers)
- Trial Counsel, *U.S. v. Butler and Rabat* and Appellate Counsel, *U.S. v. Leonard Peltier* (defense of American Indian movement members on charges stemming from 1975 shoot-out on Pine Ridge Reservation, resulting in the deaths of one Native American and two FBI agents)
- Appellate Counsel, *Texas v. Johnson and Eichmann, et. al.* (1989 and 1990 Supreme Court arguments in flag-burning cases)

With the modern media being what it is, and with Bill's expert use of it, he probably had more of an impact on more people in his time than Clarence Darrow had in his. Bill was featured on *Face the Nation*, the *Today Show, Good Morning America, 20/20, 60 Minutes, Prime Time Live*, and the *Donohue Show*, to name a few. He was a guest on countless radio programs throughout the country. He was even a member of the Screen Actors Guild, playing the role of Jim Morrison's attorney in Oliver Stone's *The Doors* and the role of the judge in Spike Lee's *Malcolm X*. Bill was also a consultant to Oliver Stone's *In The Spirit of Crazy Horse*. Bill wrote articles for dozens of law reviews and magazines. In 1941, his first book of poems came out, *Our Pleasant Vices*, which was followed by two others, *Trials and Tribulations* (1985) and *Hints and Allegations* (1994). He wrote two books on the technical aspects of legal practice, and even produced a bestseller *(The Minister and the Choir Singer*, 1964). Bill's book on the civil rights struggle of the '60s, *Deep in My Heart*, is dedicated to several hundred fellow attorneys who went south for the struggle.

Bill had no funeral. He wasn't religious. Religion to him was superstition. Being part of a sect was too narrow and confining.

The Jewish heretic who transcends Jewry belongs to a Jewish tradition. The historian Isaac Deutscher had a phrase for it, "the non-Jewish Jew." Bill, much like his colleague Len Weinglass, was in line with the great revolutionaries of modern thought: Spinoza, Heine, Marx, Luxemburg, Trotsky, Freud, and Einstein, whose photo hung in Len's Chelsea loft. These people went beyond the boundaries of Judaism, finding it too narrow, archaic, constricting.

I do not wish to stretch the comparison. Bill was not as much a radical thinker as a man of action. But his intellectual understanding—and he was extremely well educated—powered his activity. He had in common with these great thinkers the idea that knowledge, to be real, must be acted upon. As Marx observed: "Hitherto the philosophers have only interpreted the world, the point is to change it."

Like his intellectual predecessors, Bill saw reality in a state of flux, as dynamic and not static, and he was aware of the constantly changing and contradictory nature of society. Bill was essentially an optimist and shared with the great Jewish revolutionaries an optimistic belief in humanity and a belief in the solidarity of humankind.

At the end of the Civil War, when the guns were still crackling and the Union troops (many of them African American) marched in to take over the remaining Southern posts, a song was often on their lips:

> John Brown's body lies a moldering in the grave,
> John Brown's body lies a moldering in the grave,
> John Brown's body lies a moldering in the grave,
> But his truth goes marching on.

So does Bill's.

SIXTIES RADICALS: A NOTE ON THE *LAW AND DISORDER* INTERVIEWS

Mel Wulf, Peter Weiss, and Ramsey Clark are all retired now, all into their nineties. Michael Ratner, Heidi Boghosian, and I interviewed them for the "Lawyers You'll Like" segment of our radio show *Law and Disorder*. The rest of the interviewees are of that generation that got active in the 1960s.

A good proportion of the '60s radical attorneys are women. This is so because for the first time women were allowed into law schools in large numbers. There was a time in American history when there were no women lawyers. The great black feminist and civil rights attorney Florynce Kennedy had to fight for a women's restroom at Columbia Law School. When I started at New York University School of Law in 1964, 10 percent of my classmates were women. School officials bragged about that. Nowadays about half the law students at most schools are women. The movement lawyers of the '60s got political during the civil rights, anti-war, gay, and feminist movements of their times. They are now mostly in their seventies, many of them still practicing.

MICHAEL TIGAR

MICHAEL STEVEN SMITH: Today on *Law and Disorder*, we're delighted to have with us the great human rights lawyer Michael Tigar, emeritus professor of law at Duke University and at the Washington College of Law. He's been a lawyer working on social change issues since the 1960s. He's argued numerous cases in the United States Supreme Court and many circuit courts of appeal. His books include *Law and the Rise of Capitalism*, *Fighting Injustice*, and the forthcoming *Mythologies of the State and Monopoly Power*. And we're also joined by our guest co-host, attorney Jim Lafferty, former head of the Los Angeles chapter of the National Lawyers Guild.

Since 9/11, our democracy, however restricted at the time, has been even further shrunk by the growth of the national security state and the all-knowing surveillance apparatus that has been set up. Moreover, the president as the head of the executive branch of the government has gathered unto himself an unprecedented amount of power over the judicial and the legislative branches of our government.

I want to start off by asking you a question: What is law? Martin Luther King's courageous attorney, Bill Kunstler, was given an award by the New York State Association of Criminal Defense Attorneys back in 1994, as was his classmate at Columbia, Federal Judge Jack Weinstein. Kunstler spoke first, he accepted the award on behalf of his clients. Then he said what he thought the judge believed the law was.

Kunstler said he thought that the judge thought that law was the considered response of a civilized society to the problem of reaching a reasoned and intelligent conclusion to disputes between the state and its citizens or between the citizens themselves, and that's the liberals' view of the law. Kunstler said, "But my view is different." He told the audience that he thought that the law was in fundamental essence nothing more than a method of social control created by a socio-economic system determined at all costs to perpetuate itself by all and any means necessary for as long as possible. Do you share this view?

MICHAEL TIGAR: Well, he's half right but you can bat .500 and still lead the league. Of course the law is a system of rules. In my book, *Law and the Rise of Capitalism*, I talked about legal ideology, which is erect as a superstructure on a system of social relations and is designed to protect and preserve that system of social relations.

But then the next question is, how do they do it? They can have cops on every corner and they can have repressive regimes and they can crush you, or they can write something like the Constitution and the Bill of Rights, which is a set of promises the regime makes to the people about how there's going to be freedom and justice and so on. Just you wait and see, don't make too much trouble because your so-called rights are protected.

What's happened is, of course, that the set of mythologies grow up. We have a department that calls itself justice when we know exactly what the hell it's doing. We have inadequate legal services so people are pleading guilty and being hustled off to prison. But when you get a jury trial, when you get an Article 3 judge like Judge Weinstein who really cares about things, it's still possible to win these victories.

Of all people in the world, at that stage of his career, Bill Kunstler knew that because he spent his career as one of the most formidable advocates in the United States of America defending people, keeping them out of jail and all the rest of it. And you know what, if he really in his heart of hearts thought that that was complete bullshit, I don't think he'd have wasted his time.

Now then, with Judge Weinstein. It's nice to be able to characterize your opponent's position as he does with Weinstein. Weinstein was not only very smart but you know he was clever. We took to him, as a matter of fact, in 1971. Many thousands of young men had gone outside the United States to escape the draft and yet when we looked at their Selective Service files, it turned out they were never going to be drafted anyway because if they'd had good lawyers, they wouldn't have been called. They were eligible for deferments or whatever.

So, we proposed to Weinstein, "Why don't you resurrect all the Selective Service files and start deciding these cases of these young men that have been indicted for draft refusal and have left the country." Weinstein said, "Okay, I'll do that." The Second Circuit didn't agree, but this was one of the pressures that led then to the amnesty for the draft refusers.

So, I don't agree with Judge Weinstein all the time, but he understands what an Article 3 judge can do because he says, "Hey look, I'm not doing anything radical. I'm just making sure the regime keeps its promises to the people."

JIM LAFFERTY: Speaking of the judges though, you had been editor in chief of your law review at the University of California and that's an entree into some good jobs and some great clerkships. You, in fact, became a clerk to Justice William Brennan, United States Supreme Court. But you only lasted a week. What happened?

TIGAR: I actually lasted less than a week.

LAFFERTY: I was trying to be nice.

TIGAR: I didn't even get the job. Brennan appointed me as his clerk at the end of my second year in law school to take up the job when I graduated. The word got out and all hell broke loose. James Kilpatrick of the *Richmond News Leader* wrote an editorial called "The Lady and The Tiger." A member of the House Committee on Un-American Activities attacked the court. Ramsey Clark got the FBI involved in providing information to Brennan about my so-called political background.

At that time, Ronald Reagan was running for governor of California. Brennan walks into chambers one day and looks at his law clerk from the previous term, Owen Fiss. He says, "The chief told me to fire Tigar." That's [Earl] Warren. Warren was worried that maybe Ronald Reagan would become governor of California, which by the way he was going to get unless he'd been found in a motel with a male chicken.

So, Brennan got upset. We had a meeting, I flew back to Washington. We talked about it and he told me some of the things, that FBI reports had been sent to him, much of which was bullshit. I took the position that I was not going to make a public statement about my politics and I wouldn't authorize him to make one either, because we're not going to be sanitizing me. I would disclose to him anything that he wanted and he accepted that idea.

I got back to Washington and he had changed his mind and he withdrew the invitation to be his clerk. There it was. I got a job with Edward Bennett Williams. It was unusual. I argued, let's see, one, two, I guess I'd argued three cases up there by 1977 and Brennan wrote to me and asked me to come and have lunch with him and I did. His first thing out of his mouth was, "You don't know how much trouble I had getting by Byron White to be the fifth vote for you in that case." We talked back and forth and we then started to meet every once in a while. I worked with him on some speeches he wanted to make, we talked. He then wrote to me and apologized.

LAFFERTY: Finally apologized.

TIGAR: He said, "I overreacted, I'm sorry. The only thing that helps me live with myself is that we have become good friends." It's amazing, the last time I ever saw him was in chambers. We were walking out of his chambers into his office. He grabbed me by the arm and he said, "Have I done any good up here?" I said, "Yeah," which goes back to Michael Steven Smith's first question. "Have I done any good up here?"

That is the Brennan story. The bright side is that as you know, I became famous as the guy that was appointed to be a Supreme Court clerk, but I never had to read any petitions. I didn't have to do the work.

LAFFERTY: But it was on your resume.

TIGAR: Yes.

SMITH: Michael, in your book *Law and the Rise of Capitalism*, you propose what you call an insurgent role for lawyers. Talk about what this means please.

TIGAR: I used the term "Jurisprudence of Insurgency." That is the same saying with which we started today. There are open spaces in the law. There are promises the regime has made to the people that it feels obliged to keep. And so, what Bill Kunstler did for all those years and what I hope a bunch of others of us do is we represent people and call on the state to keep those promises.

But as time goes by, it becomes clear that the state is not keeping these promises. That pandemic racism still dominates events. That we can manage to get some person in the White House who systematically commits a series of crimes and so far at least is not accountable for them and so on. That is the point at which the lawyer has to say to the clients, because it's all about the clients as you pointed out with your first question, "I'm sorry that the struggle we're doing will keep on. But, really I'm not going to over-promise about what is going to happen."

That's the Jurisprudence of Insurgency. When I was in South Africa in '88, '89, you could see that. The African National Congress conducted a two-part struggle. It had many, many lawyers who showed up and represented ANC members and sympathizers and at the same time, it had an armed struggle that went on over the years. The interesting thing, I know it's a long answer. Nineteen eighty-nine, I'm sitting with Dullah Omar, who was Mandela's lawyer. Later became minister of justice.

We were over there, Ken Brown, Jim Ferguson, and I training young lawyers and he said, "Tomorrow, I want you to teach these lawyers how to cross-examine cops." I said, "Okay, I can do that." "I need a demonstration," he said, "because what we're going to do this summer, we have a new organization. We're going to have wait-ins, sit-ins, walk-ins, and so on. People of color are majority in this country. We're going to bring the place to a halt and nobody's going to plead guilty. They're all going to be mass arrests and we're going to cross-examine every cop, we're going to try every case, and Mandela's coming out."

I said, "Dullah, this is just bullshit. I've seen the dogs, I've seen the guns. I've seen the whole thing." He said, "No, he's coming out. We're going to just show our power in this way and bring the system to a halt." And as you know, Mandela got out.

LAFFERTY: He was right.

TIGAR: He was right, but that's the sort of interplay of an understanding of the laws of motion of a social system and its legal ideology and the prospect of change.

LAFFERTY: If a law student came to you today, asked you for some counseling, said, "Look Professor Tigar, I understand Karl Marx studied law, Fidel Castro, Lenin were both lawyers for a short time but then they joined Socialist, activist organizations. I'm wondering what I should do. I'm a Socialist as a young law student here. Should I be getting out of law school and getting into one of these Socialist organizations or should I stick it out in law school, practice law? I feel conflict now."

TIGAR: Well, the first thing that I would say is you ought to learn your craft. That is to say, learn what they got for you, because you'll never be able to replicate that experience. You've got clinical legal education opportunities actually to learn how to relate with clients and to deal with their concerns, because I'll tell you something as I wrote in a play once. I had a character say, "You lawyers imagine you stand at the center of all the events by which the world is moved," which of course is not true.

You stand where you stand when you stand because some client is a victim of injustice. But that's the definition of a trial lawyer, a massive blob of ego suspended over a chasm of insecurity. But what I would tell this lawyer is, you've got some options. One thing is, you could be a professor, write books, and be influential. You could sort of emulate the young Karl Marx whose iconic essays on the law would still resonate.

Or, you could be a trial lawyer. Because, you might think the law is bullshit and maybe it is, but when some client calls you from the jail and says, "Could you come down and get me out?" That puts an obligation on you to get that job done and maybe try that case to a jury and make a deal.

LAFFERTY: And that might be a political activist of great importance at the moment.

TIGAR: The third thing you can do is, you can become involved in human rights litigation because they're still doing it. And now and at the risk of wasting your time, I'll tell you a story. Forty years ago, Orlando Letelier and Ronni Moffitt were assassinated in Washington, D.C. at Sheridan Circle by agents of the Chilean secret police, the DINA. The actual assassin was Michael Vernon Townley, a joint citizen of Chile and the United States.

He gets put in the Witness Protection Program and is still being run as an intelligence agent 'til this good day. We get a judgment against Chile for Isabel the widow and her sons, and we collected $4 million. Well, Townley also killed somebody else. In 1973 during the coup, he killed a Spanish diplomat named Carmelo Soria in Santiago. So, my students, the human rights clinic that Jane and I run, we sued Townley for killing Carmelo Soria in Santiago and we get a default judgment against him.

Now, the widow of Carmelo, Laura González-Vera, starts a lawsuit in Chile saying, "I want Chile to extradite Townley out of the United States, get him back here and try him." Well, I went down and I appear before a single justice of the Chilean Supreme Court and he says, "No." He said, "I'm very sorry, but the amnesty that Pinochet granted to his people extends to Townley and we can't try him for murder here because he got amnesty."

So, we went downstairs and we did law student stuff. I said to my students, I said, "You know something, the Chilean penal code has a different crime called illicit association. It's not conspiracy, it's the commission of substantive offenses while a member of an illicit group." Townley worked with a group of people who carried out these terrible things. So, we go to the Chilean Supreme Court, all the justices, and take a daring position.

The Chilean Supreme Court for the first time holds that the entire Pinochet secret police apparatus was an illicit association and opens the door to prosecuting and civil suits in Chile where the situation is. And you know what, it was law students from Washington College of Law who did the research and met with Laura González-Vera and worked with these human rights lawyers and so on.

So, what would I tell that young man? I'd say to that young person, I'd say, "Well you know, there's still work to do. Me, I'm kind of getting too old for this. I'm like the dog on the porch that used to bark at cars." I bark at injustices.

SMITH: I'm reminded of what Hillary Clinton said about her husband. He's a hard dog to keep on the porch. Michael, you, me, and Jim are all around the same age. We're all '60s radicals. You were active in the anti-Vietnam War movement in Berkeley, California when you were a student at the University of California. Jim and I were active in the anti-war movement in Detroit.

I wanted to ask you about the challenges that we face today as compared to back then fifty years ago. We were able to lend a hand and of course, it was the Vietnamese that really did it, but we were able to lend a hand in stopping the American aggression against Vietnam. We were able to lend a hand in the impeachment of Richard Nixon. And now, we're embroiled in the forever war. It looks like Trump is likely to not be impeached, although I'm not sure. But, how would you compare the period back then when we were young and active and the period now?

TIGAR: In the Vietnam War period we had, it's funny to say this, the advantage that millions of young men felt the pressure of the draft. Now, that was both a blessing and not a blessing because some of them thought that if you just opposed the draft as opposed to looking at imperialism and its manifestations of the broader look, that you'd done enough. But the fact is that the resistance to the draft, the wholesale resistance to the draft was a major factor.

And indeed talking about the legal thing, first case I ever argued in the Supreme Court of the United States was in 1969. I was twenty-eight years old. The Selective Service System, if you tore up your draft card, they classified you as delinquent and immediately accelerated you for induction. Three thousand young men had gone to jail on that basis. The Supreme Court held unanimously that that was illegal and those three thousand young men got out.

How the court changed its view over a couple of terms, I don't know. But, those were the days. What's going on today? What we're seeing is, I think, a very impressive civil rights movement around the issue of racism because that racism is a major pandemic, major issue. The attitude of this administration toward the far right and the fascists is a big deal. That's the most hopeful sign here.

Whether Trump's going to be impeached or not, I don't know. I don't think we can always . . . We shouldn't put our faith in the government to solve our problems for us. In addition to that, these promises that are being made about bringing jobs back to the United States and so forth and so on, okay, we're seeing some bump in the unemployment figures that looks good. But the fact is, that this wholesale business of globalization, outsourcing and so on is going to come back to bite the administration on the ass just as it did the Democrats for supporting all these things that permitted exporting jobs to other countries.

LAFFERTY: And even those unemployment figures. People are taking two or three jobs to survive having no medical benefits, no guaranteed hours. I mean, it's high unemployment of poverty-level jobs in many cases.

SMITH: With respect to the power of the executive. Even at the time of the founding of our country and the writing of the Constitution, there was a fear that the executive branch of the government would be too powerful because the president controlled the military. Are the powers of the executive larger now than they were in the '60s? And conversely, has the power of the legislative branch of the government been diminished?

TIGAR: Your concern about what the founding fathers thought is exactly right. Patrick Henry opposed adoption of the Constitution because he said if your chief executive be a man of address and he comes at the head of his army, will Mr. Chief Justice make him give bail? So, he understood the problem.

But, let's fast forward to your concern. Here we get this massive surveillance and the first thing we know about it is that it is everything, they're collecting everything. Second thing we know about it is, it's secret. This is a secret process. You can't even know what they're doing.

But, what we do know they're doing is, they're sneaking some of that information off to law enforcement people who are using it to prosecute folks and to make untraceable the illegal sources of the information. Second, they're using it to program drone strikes, which have killed thousands of civilians despite their claims about accuracy. The first thing that happens is, that's what they're doing.

Now, the second thing that happens is that the judicial branch does not step up to the task. This is one of these times we reached the end point. Does not step up to the task of providing any redress. The judicial branch accepts the state secrets privilege, which is not like the lawyer-client privilege. That protects your privacy. The state's secret privilege counterpoises the state to the interest of the citizens in knowing what's going on.

And so, you have a drone strike that kills an American citizen who is targeted and that person is told, that family is told first, we can't even discuss this in court because the whole thing is secret. The second thing is, well it's a political question and the courts really can't address it. So, the judiciary abdicates in the face of claims by the executive branch that the courts have no business.

SMITH: There's been a lot written in recent times since the Patriot Act about how many of the first ten amendments, that is, the Bill of Rights, have been eroded.

TIGAR: Well, let's start with Amendment Number One, freedom of speech. Not so much eroded as subjected to a pervasive mythology that renders it much less effective than you would've thought. I have a book coming out in September, *Mythologies of State and Monopoly Power*. I begin one chapter by saying, "I walked down to the marketplace of ideas the other day, but they didn't have anything I wanted. I went over to the side, there were some actual people that had some ideas. They were passing out leaflets, but the cops are running them off."

The fact is that it used to be that you could stand in a street corner and pass out leaflets. It used to be, if you wanted to organize a union, get into the plant. Supreme Court said, "No." Go to the shopping center, "Sorry, that's private property." It looks like a city, it's portrayed as a city, it's a simulacrum of a city, it's a gathering place but I'm sorry, you've got to stand next to the freeway and pass out your leaflets.

We've got a case like Citizens United. A perfectly good Supreme Court justice like Anthony Kennedy decides that corporations have First Amendment rights. Now, the Supreme Court, when it held that corporations could be criminally liable, pointed out that corporations have enormous power that transcends that of any private individual. So, why would you equate the right of the individual hand biller to that?

Then, back in the day, we had a thing called the Fairness Doctrine. Why? Because the ether, the broadcast spectrum, that's up there in the sky. Nobody can own it. It is a limited resource, but broadcasters said, "No, no, no. We own the actual radio station, the hardware. That must mean that we're the ones that communicate." And thus the Supreme Court's decision in the famous Red Lion case is no more. I don't know if you remember that case.

Fred Cook, who was a great investigative journalist, was attacked by Billy James Hargis, Reverend Billy James Hargis. Cook demanded the right of reply and the station said no. Supreme Court upheld the Fairness Doctrine and said he had the right of reply. That was a great case because Hargis then got into trouble because of financial and sexual peccadilloes that he . . . It was said that he had sex with both the bride and the groom on the wedding night after he performed the ceremony, but we don't know if they each got equal time.

SMITH: Let's talk about the Supreme Court now that Justice Kennedy is leaving and it looks like his chosen replacement, Brett Kavanaugh, is going to step up to the job. I wanted to get your feelings about what we now have is a five to four hard-right majority on the Supreme Court. What kind of cases do you think are coming up before them and how do you think they might decide these cases? There was the originalist doctrine that Judge Scalia propounded.

There was the other doctrine Chief Justice Roberts said that he only calls balls and strikes, that he doesn't make the law. What do you think of these doctrines that the Supreme Court is now propounding?

TIGAR: Well, it's nonsense. It's been nonsense ever since at least the Adams administration, because the Adams administration understood that you had to control the judiciary. That's why they passed the Midnight Judges Act, that's how we got John Marshall as chief justice. Anybody that reads American history knows that that's just nonsense and John Roberts doesn't believe it either.

Now, with respect to originalism, that too is a fiction because we cannot know the mindset of those folks and even if we . . . Some of the hints that we have about them, that is to say they owned slaves and that they thought that white men of property were the only people eligible to jury service, and all the rest of that stuff that was regarded as the way things were at the time the Constitution was adopted, we simply don't accept anymore.

LAFFERTY: Here's what's always fascinated me and I want you to talk about. Even when people point to the Federalist Papers, they quote it with great authority or this and that as part of the originalist idea, that's an interpretation. They're still making an interpretation.

TIGAR: Well, Madison himself said, "Who knows what future generations will make of the words that we have written." That by the way is originalist. It was Madison by the way who also warned about the excesses, the executive branch, saying that, "We hope that we have rejected the impious doctrine of the old world that people are made for kings and not kings for people." So, originalism is silly.

It's simply a cover for an agenda that folks have. I think Justice Kennedy himself said from time to time that he was an originalist. Nonetheless, he wrote leading opinions on the right of gay marriage and all the rest of it. He wasn't really an originalist.

The court is corporate. They've tried to curb the power of unions again with this phony First Amendment argument. It becomes a challenge, so we ask ourselves. You go up there, there are nine justices. You ask yourself, "How do I get five votes?" With Roberts, what kinds of issues am I likely to be able to get a vote? On the right to counsel in criminal cases, he's written some interesting things.

If we've got that case, that's the one to whom we're speaking and with Scalia, he came on the bench. He had already made up his mind. There was no sense talking to him. All he wanted to do was interrupt your argument and be rude to you. So, we're in a bad spot. What could I say? But, I want to remind you, apartheid shut down the black vote in South Africa in 1953. For thirty years those lawyers went to court every day and defended people. They kept the faith and kept up the struggle.

LAFFERTY: It's also worth noting in that same regard, that the all-male Supreme Court that thought a woman had no right to choose didn't simply wake up one morning and say, "Geez have we been schmucks, of course she has a right to choose." Hundreds of thousands of people over and over again marched in the streets, went to jail, made it so that politics that we talk about suddenly began to turn the other way on the court, didn't it?

TIGAR: Well, you can see that in a number of instances. One of my favorites is, after the civil rights movement became tired of suing one school district, one grade at a time, in 1960, February first, the sit-in movement begins in Greensboro and then the Direct Action Movement. And all of a sudden, the lawyer's role was transformed into representing folks in criminal courts and whoops, the world changes.

Early 1963 I think, the first wave of sit-in cases reaches the Supreme Court. Solicitor General Cox files an amicus brief pointing out how the Jim Crow system was installed in the South and so on. The court writes an opinion that basically exonerates the people who had sat-in.

The thousands of young people that had put their bodies on the line about civil rights, the court said, "Look, we could go through this case by case. We could look at this . . . But no, tell you what. The passage of the Civil Rights Act abates all those prosecutions, reset the clock to zero. Start over again." Same thing I think with that Selective Service case that I talked about.

One of the things I learned sitting in a law office in Washington, D.C. was that people that were ordinarily very conservative, either they or their friends had young men who were subject to the draft. It's like being told you're being hanged in the morning, it just clarifies your vision.

SMITH: The Far Right led by the Koch brothers and their network of billionaires are very strategic. Since 2010, they've elected seven hundred people to state legislatures. Ultimately, they would like a constitutional amendment coming out of a constitutional convention under Article Five, which would allow for two thirds of the states to call a convention and amend the Constitution with two thirds of the states voting for it and some other things, but they could get over that and they could amend our constitution.

This was done by the military dictator Pinochet in Chile about whom you've spoken and I know you're familiar with him. They altered the Constitution in Chile in such a way as to almost permanently preserve the property rights of the ultra rich of that country. Do you see that there's a danger of this happening here in the United States?

TIGAR: Absolutely. I think that the danger of, let's call it fascism because that's what it is and the danger that rich folks like the Koch brothers or however you pronounce it taking charge of the political process through the unlimited supply of money that the Supreme Court now holds they can pump into the process creates this real and present danger. So yes, that exists. Then the question is, what should we do about it?

Now, Chile at the time of the Pinochet coup had a strong left tradition. Those folks mobilized and eventually succeeded in pushing him from office and because of the work I did with some other people, I got to see some of that. So the question is, yes these are the dangers. This is what these folks want to do. What should we do about it? What we should do about it is, don't mourn, organize.

Everybody in their own community has the opportunity to do something. The two people to whom I was speaking can do something, you do this radio program. I happen to live in North Carolina. My wife calls our two senators every other day and points out that, "How can you apologize and be an apologist for and not stand up to a man who violates every conservative traditional value that you purport to uphold?"

I am amazed at the number of law students and law schools who want to get involved in doing human rights clinical work and provide representation to the unrepresented. I mean, if you're in a law school and you're listening to me right now, go look up the clinical programs and see what you can do. And if they don't have one, then go to the local Prisoners' Rights Office and People's Law Office and all the rest of it and ask your professors if you can get course credit for going to work in there.

So, we each do what we can and we recognize that the three of us that are around here, I don't know how old we all are, but I don't think we're going to see how this ultimately plays out. We just keep doing what we can.

SMITH: The Center for Constitutional Rights president Jules Lobel wrote a significant book, *Success Without Victory*. In it he says, "The law generally is designed to maintain the status quo and maintain state power but it is a tension, particularly in modern capitalism. The power is maintained through the use of laws that can't be used by the oppressed to challenge that power. The key task for social movement lawyers therefore it is to empower people, to help build movements, and to challenge in fundamental ways how state power is used." I assume you agree with that, but how might lawyers do that today? Is it any different doing it today than it was when you started doing it so many, many, many years ago?

TIGAR: Yes and no. We try cases the same way that Abe Lincoln tried cases. We cross-examine snitches, we cross-examine cops, we ask the court to provide us information that we say that the other side is withholding. These are the basic techniques that we use. Second, we recur, as Jules Lobel says, to the fundamental principles about what I've characterized as the promises the regime makes to the people.

The law books, our people, are full of cases in which we can cite to the Supreme Court to this good day pointing out that the court has a job to do and ought to get busy and do it. They're also full of horrible cases. Indeed it was some of those horrible cases in the McCarthy period that led me to want to go to law school.

SMITH: Is it tougher though? Is it tougher today to be that movement lawyer than it was then, or is it different in some ways if not tougher? I'm thinking, I suppose, of the sophistication of the surveillance.

TIGAR: It is hard to convince judges to penetrate the wall of secrecy and surveillance. But learning your craft and keeping on the track is there but also, there are fewer barriers to entry to being an effective lawyer than there were fifty years ago. That is to say, fifty years ago if you wanted to start an office, you had to have books. You had to have space for the books. You needed all kinds of paralegal, secretarial help and so on. These days, for $800 from Best Buy or wherever the heck it is, you can buy a computer and a printer and you get a low cost subscription to some online legal services or any bar associations—you have cheaper ones that are included in your dues, like the D.C. bar does. Now, with a ream of paper, you're in business. In terms of barriers to entry and in terms of the cost of maintaining your office, it's less.

The second thing is that you begin to start exploring fee-shifting arrangements like the Equal Access to Justice Act if you begin doing civil cases. Getting appointed to represent people in criminal cases and arguing for continuing to raise the hourly rate and the number of hours for which you can bill. That by the way is difficult. There's a judge out in the Eighth Circuit that kept denying. He said, "Listen, I am not going to allow you to pay for running down there and visiting your client in the jail. Have them come to your office." It was pointed out that these are capital cases and it was very unlikely that the client was going to be able to come to your office.

SMITH: Much as he might wish to.

TIGAR: I get that now. Sometimes it's like trying to explain a sundial to a bat, but you can succeed so yes, there is opportunity. It's a different form of legal organization. Second, for you at the top of the class who have these aspirations, major law firms are much more conscious of the need to do pro bono work.

For example a year ago, Erdogan's thugs beat up some Kurdish demonstrators in Washington. Well, we've got two law firms working with law students at Washington School of Law. We're suing Turkey and the actual goons, but law firms are putting their young associates on that to learn about this and to participate in the process because it makes them better lawyers. The answer could go on and on, but the message is clear. Nobody has an excuse to sit on the sidelines and bemoan the lack of opportunity to get involved.

HAYWOOD BURNS (1940–1996)

He represented Dr. Martin Luther King Jr. in the Poor People's Campaign in the 1960s. King was murdered in Memphis but Haywood came through unscathed. He represented Angela Davis, successfully defending her against a frame-up charge of murder and kidnapping. He organized the defense of the Attica brothers, charging Governor Nelson A. Rockefeller with the responsibility for "human tragedy that ranks in the annals of national disgrace with My Lai." He fought apartheid in the 1980s and the 1990s when repression in South Africa peaked. He helped found the National Conference of Black Lawyers (NCBL) to "represent the Black Revolution."

But such is the irony of history that, in Cape Town, South Africa, after the dust over the apartheid regime had settled, Haywood Burns—our friend, comrade, and mentor; former National Lawyers Guild president; City University of New York law professor; and partner in the Harlem law firm of Van Lierop, Burns & Schaap—was killed by a truck running a stop sign.

Haywood was attending a conference on democracy and international law and had recently heard Nelson Mandela speak. Wilhelm Joseph was there with him and told me, "It was not just hearing Mandela as a released prisoner, but hearing him speak as the head of state, that caused Haywood to reflect that it 'was the happiest day of my life.'"

Driving to the funeral at the Abyssinian Baptist Church, I recalled to Hal Mayerson the time he had introduced Haywood as "the *consigliore* of the Left." It was funny the way Hal had put it, but nonetheless true. More than anyone in our circle, Haywood was respected for his kindness and accomplishments; more than anyone, Haywood was imbued with the moral authority of a leader. "Haywood could argue the most radical of causes with the lightest of touches," said Danny Alterman, New York president of the Guild. "We are all devastated. He touched so many lives in the progressive community."

Haywood had a natural dignity and handsomeness. I teased him one time reminding him of his resemblance to Karl Marx, whose children, well-steeped in Shakespeare, had called him "the Moor." Haywood smiled back and suggested Frederick Douglass as well. I remember Haywood on two occasions quoting from Douglass that "power concedes nothing without a demand, it never did and it never will." I couldn't remember the entire quote, but Haywood did.

Haywood was representing a fellow NCBL member, Robert Ellis, against the First Judicial Departmental Disciplinary Committee when he died. Ellis had publicly criticized Supreme Court County Acting Justice Daniel P. Fitzgerald for putting his client in prison pending appeal. The judge invariably remanded those who were convicted and since these persons were usually black and Latino, Ellis observed that this was a racist practice.

Haywood had been making the point that "it is unnecessary to denominate a person a 'racist' to get at racist practices" for three decades, most recently in testimony before a Second Circuit task force on racism in the courts. He came to Ellis's defense, submitting a forty-page brief just before he died. Our Guild chapter has also been working in support of Ellis and has submitted a legal letter in his defense.

The New York City chapter of the National Lawyers Guild named a mentoring program for law students after Haywood. A new elementary school in Manhattan has been named the Haywood Burns School. Children from that institution sang at a CUNY Law School graduation ceremony, which I attended. Hearing those songs, I reflected on the impact Haywood was able to make and recalled a Stephen Spender poem about extraordinary people. The truly great,

Spender thought, were those who had remembered the soul's history from the womb, and

> . . . Whose lovely ambition
> Was that their lips, still touched with fire,
> Should tell of their Spirit, clothed from head to foot in song.

JIM LAFFERTY

James T. (Jim) Lafferty (b. 1938) was a national leader in the 1960s of the American movement against the war in Vietnam. He practiced law in Detroit, where he pioneered the defense of draft resisters. He was a founding partner of the Detroit movement law firm Lafferty, Reosti, Jabara, James, Papakhian, Stickgold, Smith, and Soble. Prior to that he served as executive director of the National Lawyers Guild and spent time in Mississippi during the civil rights movement. He founded the Oakland County Chapter of the American Civil Liberties Union before moving to New York City, and then Los Angeles, where he became the head of the Los Angeles Chapter of the National Lawyers Guild.

MICHAEL STEVEN SMITH: Jim, by way of introduction and by way of full disclosure, I've known you for almost forty-five years. We go all the way back to Detroit. Biographically, listeners should know that you went to the University of Michigan in the '50s and then Wayne State University Law School. You were working for the first racially integrated law firm in the country, the Goodman and Crockett firm.

How did you come to work for the Goodman and Crockett firm? What kind of firm was it, and what brought you there?

JIM LAFFERTY: That is actually kind of an interesting story. My wife and I had befriended a woman who was divorced. She was white. She divorced a white fellow, married an African American surgeon, and then the woman's mother and former husband moved to take away the child, thinking the child should not be raised in a bi-racial home.

This was 1958, in Detroit, Michigan. It later went on to become a movie called *One Potato, Two Potato*. This woman needed a lawyer, so I asked my law school professor, the one African American law school professor we had, who would take this case? And he said, "You need George Crockett." Crockett was an African American lawyer who had integrated the firm that you mentioned: Goodman, Crockett, Eden, Robin, and Filo. George agreed to take the case. The case ultimately was lost all the way through the Michigan Supreme Court, in the course of which I had researched every child-custody case that ever had been decided by the court. There was absolutely no basis except race for denying this woman her child after she had married an African American man. But nevertheless, that's what the courts ruled, including the Michigan Supreme Court. She did lose custody of the child, and eventually, by the way, committed suicide.

SMITH: And that was your introduction to the Goodman Crockett firm.

LAFFERTY: It was. And then they hired me as a law clerk.

SMITH: And listeners should know that that was the main firm in Michigan. It had been founded with the rise of the United Automobile Workers and the rise of the CIO. Maurice Sugar, who was the attorney for the Automobile Workers, was the founder of that firm. It was the great civil rights, civil liberties firm in the country. Because they had a connection with the Lawyers Guild, they were like the leaders of the Lawyers Guild. Ernie Goodman was a founding member. And that got you the nod to become the executive director of the National Lawyers Guild. You had the job that Heidi Boghosian has now.

LAFFERTY: Well, therefore I understand what Heidi's going through today. It's not an easy job. It's a wonderful organization, but a tough job. You can imagine being the head of an organization of lawyers and law students and legal workers; what could be a bigger nightmare anyway? Even if they're wonderful people. Those were wonderful years, though, in the Guild. We didn't have time to be fighting with each other because you had the civil rights movement in the South.

We set up an office in the South and we took depositions, we defended. That's, I think, one of the proudest chapters in the National Lawyers Guild's history. That answering of the call by principally a white organization, the Lawyers Guild, going down into the South where there were only two lawyers in Mississippi and Alabama between them who would take these cases.

HEIDI BOGHOSIAN: Could you explain Arthur Kinoy's role, and explain who he is for listeners?

LAFFERTY: Arthur Kinoy, also one of the early members of the Guild, went on to become a very famous law professor at Rutgers. He always tells the great story about how, at a 1963 convention of the Guild, he gets a phone call from Len Holt, an African American, one of the two lawyers in the South handling these cases. Arthur says to him, "Len, where are you?" And Len says, "The question is, Arthur, where are you? And why aren't you down here in Mississippi with me?" And he came back into the convention, proposed to the National Lawyers Guild convention on the spot that we scrap everything else that we were doing, forget the agenda; the civil rights movement in the South is calling and we need to answer that call. And I'm proud to say we did.

DALIA HASHAD: Tell us about why you became a lawyer.

LAFFERTY: Well, that's a very unromantic story. I never could stop talking in school. My mother spent more time in school, I think, than I did because I was constantly being thrown out of school. I had a teacher I much loved who looked at me one day and said, "Jimmy, you should be a lawyer when you grow up. You have a gift for gab." And she was trying to silence me at the time. And no one in my family had ever gone to school or college or anything, and that was the first time anybody ever said anything halfway encouraging. So I thought, "Well, all right. I'm not sure what a lawyer is, but I guess so." And then I think, to be a little more serious about it, I think partly having to do with stories around my own family and upbringing, I had a clear sense of injustice.

It bothered me, whether it was visited upon me or anyone else. So at an early age, I think because of that, I transferred happily in a good direction.

HASHAD: It seems pretty immediately in the direction of racial justice.

LAFFERTY: Yeah—Racial justice; religious justice. I was the only non-Jewish kid in my neighborhood, and then a few African American kids began to move in. It was a changing neighborhood. And you could see right away the problems that were developing in Detroit. And yet, somehow, we all got along well. But then you'd go to school, you'd see one of these kids ill-treated. And these were your buddies, and so that sense of injustice, that snapped in.

SMITH: Jim, the political movement in the '50s and the '60s for us kind of spilled over and continued with the civil rights movement, but then also got involved in opposing America's imperialist war in Vietnam. You played a role in that. Could you share some of your memories of the anti-war movement then, and what lessons you think it has for us now?

LAFFERTY: There's no standing anti-war movement the way there is a standing army. Somebody has to organize it. Somebody has to have that initial vision. Somebody has to have the political ideology that can see where the country is going, to understand the imperialist nature of that war. And that was the various left parties; they helped pull together these broad coalitions that then became coalitions of everyone from virtually every walk of life. The National Peace Action Coalition, which was one of the two major coalitions that I and others helped found. We tried admirals and generals before we were done, as well as leftists, and anarchists, and religionists, and students, and labor leaders, and so forth.

What we learned, then, of course, was the same lesson that constantly has to be re-taught, sadly: when the U.S. government is engaged in an effort to expand its imperial empire, you aren't going to be able to stop that by electing somebody who is a little less imperialistic, somebody who is a little more willing to talk about peace, someone who's a little less quick to pull the trigger. You're only going to force that Congress to get out of Vietnam, or now to get out of Iraq, if you have such a mass movement from the population itself that it leaves Congress, be it Republican or Democrat, no choice. I mean, we tend to forget, for example, that we got out of Vietnam under Nixon and Ford. These were hardly men of peace. But by that time, because of the anti-war movement, both within the armed services itself—the people like you Mike and others helped build within the services itself—and the massive protests of people in the streets of America, it became impossible for anyone, including a Republican Congress or a Republican president, to continue the war anymore.

And by the way, one of the things that irritates me is people often say, "Where's the anti-war movement today? Where's the anti-war movement today?" It took twenty thousand body bags during Vietnam before a majority of the American people were opposed to the war in Vietnam. And it took more years of fighting and dying in Vietnam before you could get hundreds of thousands of people in the streets the way we've already done in this country today. The Vietnam Syndrome is alive and well in many ways. The anti-war movement today, for all of its problems, is way ahead even of where it was then—and it was a brilliant, wonderful, successful movement then.

HASHAD: Tell us about your work helping to found the National Peace Action Coalition.

LAFFERTY: Well, we founded it because by that time, the other existing coalition was drifting away somewhat from street demonstrations and was also becoming multi-issue. That is to say, it was taking up not only issues of the war, but the thirty-hour work week, and many other worthy causes. Domestic issues as well. We felt, those of us who formed the National Peace Action Coalition, that the most effective way to build a movement against the war was to require people, if they were going to join it, to only have to agree on the issue of the war.

It was easier to get people to come together if all they had to do was agree on that one central issue. And then we simply went through the campuses, as people do today, extended an invitation to everyone to join. And there was no hurdle to joining. If you were opposed to the war, we were the place to come to.

BOGHOSIAN: An important theme that has pervaded not only the Guild's history, but the history of this country, has been government overreaching.

One court case that comes to mind is U.S. District Court, the Nixon wire-tapping. Arthur Kinoy argued that case, and I believe one of the justices really chastised the government, the Nixon administration at that time, for intimidating anyone who criticized the government. And really operating their own separate system of justice. How does that relate to where we are today with eavesdropping? Do you see things as parallel to forty years ago? Or are they worse?

LAFFERTY: Oh, I think they're much worse. I was ultimately subpoenaed before the House Un-American Activities Committee, but that was near the end of its reign, and we organized a defense committee and they ultimately backed down. It's much worse today. We've got COINTELPRO today, we've got all the same kinds of stuff we had during the '60s and '70s and '50s. But more so, more so. To the extent that we expect success in the period ahead in the courts, I think we're largely kidding ourselves. I think we're going to have to rely on ourselves a lot more than we rely on the courts.

BOGHOSIAN: The movement in the streets, in other words.

LAFFERTY: The movement in the streets. Somebody asked me the other day, "What is the most effective way to stand up to the repression in this country today?" To call it what it is. To stand up on a public street corner and say, "I'm not going to take repression." To speak out against it. I mean, I think that is more effective than anything else you can do. If we won't be cowed by it, we won't need to worry about going to court over it. Now, we still need great lawyers that we have in the Guild to be doing that, to carry on that fight in the court, to win what we can win in the courts. But if we leave it to the lawyers, we're doomed. I really believe that.

Jim Lafferty was interviewed on Law and Disorder *on August 27, 2007, by Michael Ratner, Michael Steven Smith, Heidi Boghosian, and Dalia Hashad. This interview has been edited and condensed.*

MARA VERHEYDEN-HILLIARD

Attorney Mara Verheyden-Hilliard is a constitutional litigator and the co-founder in 1994 of the Partnership for Civil Justice Legal Defense and Education Fund based in Washington, D.C.

Her work involves resisting the criminalization of dissent, surveillance, data mining, and FBI harassment. The Partnership for Civil Justice Fund has had many victories, most notably the settlement of a class action lawsuit concerning the illegality of mass arrests of some seven hundred protesters and others at the April 15, 2000 demonstration in Washington, D.C. She has been the co-chair of the National Lawyers Guild Mass Defense Committee.

HEIDI BOGHOSIAN: Over the past few years and especially the past few months, the Partnership for Civil Justice Fund has had some truly landmark victories, especially in the area of protecting the right to dissent. We really wanted to find out how you got into this type of work. Tell us a bit about your background and how you came to do, specifically, the protest-related cases.

MARA VERHEYDEN-HILLIARD: Well, as you said, I co-founded the Partnership for Civil Justice and that was in 1994 with Carl Messineo, and we decided that we wanted to do this type of work—specifically, constitutional rights, economic justice, and public interest litigation—in a particular way. We didn't see other opportunities existing out there to do really what we very much felt needed to be done, and what we wanted to do. We began this work and this organization right after we left law school.

We undertook some of the longest running protest cases that we've had, in particular the recently settled class action from the April 2000 mass arrest; that's a ten-year-long case. We became involved in that case, working with other National Lawyers Guild attorneys and law students and legal workers.

MICHAEL STEVEN SMITH: Mara, where did you go to law school?

VERHEYDEN-HILLIARD: I went to Columbia Law School in New York.

SMITH: Were you political before you went to law school? Where did you get your politics?

VERHEYDEN-HILLIARD: I grew up in Washington, D.C., and I spent my childhood going to civil rights demonstrations, anti-war demonstrations, having our house filled with demonstrators. Both of my parents are deeply political people who care very much about civil rights and liberation struggles and women's rights. I was fighting these issues in my elementary school, in fact. I went to Hampshire College. After that I did women's rights work before I went to law school. I chose to go to law school specifically because there were issues I wanted to fight and things I wanted to do that I felt I wanted a law degree to be able to do them.

SMITH: How did you feel about law school?

VERHEYDEN-HILLIARD: I think honestly that law school is at least two years too long. I think that people should be able to get a law degree and become practicing lawyers, particularly if they want to be people's lawyers, by going to law school to learn the basics but then being able to actually do the work. I think that the best education that I had was actually doing the work, and the time that I spent being able to intern and clerk for different organizations and to see practical day-to-day, nuts-and-bolts litigation.

BOGHOSIAN: Now, Mara, you're known for your litigation. Tell us what your approach is in terms of not compromising, for example, protesters' rights and values.

VERHEYDEN-HILLIARD: The core of the work that we do is that we recognize the underlying social justice movements and what their ultimate goals are for human liberation. When we take on a case, a free speech case, for example, we're looking not just at a technical violation of the First Amendment, not just merely that someone's rights have been violated. And as important and critical as it is, as we stand to defend the Bill of Rights, that there are also larger issues, and that we want to keep the streets and the sidewalks and the parklands open, because all social change, all historical change in the United States that has made a difference for people, has come from below.

It has come from popular movements and popular struggle, not because the politicians decide to give people rights, but because there is that feeling that the people are demanding them and that they are going to force it to happen. So that at the end of the day, we don't see the issue being just, "do we get a judge on the bench to agree with us and that's it," it's also making sure that there is space for people to be able to express themselves. In that way, we turn to our clients again and again to make sure that we are working both with our clients and with community organizations in service of their ultimate struggle.

BOGHOSIAN: You're reminding me of Arthur Kinoy, long-time Guild member, who was sort of a hero of many Guild members. And, in fact, what Arthur told legions of law students and young lawyers is that you have to listen to the people you're serving. We take their message from them. So often traditional attorneys will advise clients in a certain way, but I think that you and Carl and the partnership really are fabulous listeners.

Knowing that these cases do take, as you say, upward of ten years and even more, I would suppose that many attorneys might be tempted to take shortcuts. Can you give some pointers for how you hang in there for the long haul in this kind of case?

VERHEYDEN-HILLIARD: First of all, I have to say, we have fabulous plaintiffs and clients. We are so honored to be able to work with people who are absolutely committed to the underlying issues, the issues that they went on the streets for to begin with, and then the issues that arise in the context of litigation. So that in these cases, for example, these two long-running mass arrest cases that we've been litigating, one since 2001, one since 2002, that we've recently settled in the past year, our clients said to us whenever we communicated with them that their ultimate goal was to make sure that what happened to them never happened to anyone else.

In both these cases where there's more than a thousand people, class members that we're representing, who were engaged in peaceful protest in Washington, D.C., and the police came in and surrounded them and swept people off the streets, took parents and their children, separating them, took protesters, took bystanders, tourists, held them on buses in punitive abusive conditions with their hands tied up behind them and then took them to a police gym floor where they were hog-tied. People were tied up wrist-to-ankle in stress and duress positions for more than twenty-four hours, unable to extend their backs.

The sadism and cruelty of this is extreme coming from the police department and ratified by the municipality, but all of our clients wanted to fight these cases out to make sure that we could change the landscape in D.C., and that's what we set out to do.

That's what the fight goes on so long for, because I think that the municipalities, the governments, they want these cases to go on as long as possible. They want to fight a war of attrition because they want plaintiffs to feel like they have to take toothless settlements and walk away with little that they've accomplished. They want to make it hard for them to find attorneys who are willing to stay and fight for the decade that it takes.

We were willing to do that, our clients were willing to do that. For example, in D.C., it has changed here. Not to say that we don't think, with an upsurge of social justice movements, that the police won't violate the law again in some way and we'll be in court that day. But the fact is right now the laws have changed in D.C. We have training in place, we've changed the way the police operate, they can't use these tactics; these specific tactics that we took apart piece by piece have been removed from the arsenal of the police department in D.C.

BOGHOSIAN: Mara, can you talk specifically about the changes to the manual that the police use for how they treat demonstrators?

VERHEYDEN-HILLIARD: Well, there were two elements of change. In a number of our cases, we've had more than those two mass arrest cases. In a series of cases we've brought over the past decade, we have as part of equitable relief gotten changes in the police mass demonstration manual, their training programs, and their requirements. As well, there was a change in the law which goes beyond the manual—in 2004 and which took effect in 2005—which is the First Amendment Rights and Police Standards Act.

That law specifically tracked the demands we were making in our cases so that, for example, the police can't just throw up these pop-up police lines and surround demonstrators and stop a demonstration, not allow people to leave, arrest them. They can't use that trap-and-detain, trap-and-arrest tactic. They can't hold people for long periods of time. If people are arrested in D.C. for basic nonviolent offenses in the context of First Amendment activity, they have to be let out in four hours now, if they're arrested by the D.C. police. They cannot use that wrist-to-ankle handcuffing mechanism against people anymore, and there are a number of other provisions like that. The police have to have their badges plainly available and visible, they can't come out in riot gear to First Amendment assemblies, which make assemblies look like they're criminal activity when, in fact, it's cherished free speech activity.

BOGHOSIAN: And also ratchets up the palpable feeling of fear among protesters.

VERHEYDEN-HILLIARD: It's an effort to demonize the protesters. One, to send a chill to protesters, but the other, to send a message to everyone else who might think, "You know, I care about this issue. I want to go out and I want to stand up for what I believe in." But then you look at it and you think, "Maybe it's dangerous?" It shouldn't appear to be dangerous to go out and speak your mind.

BOGHOSIAN: Do you think FBI intimidation and repression of activists is getting worse?

VERHEYDEN-HILLIARD: Since 2001, being a Muslim in the United States or Arab American has been, basically, to wear a target when it comes to federal law enforcement and often local law enforcement. There have been raids going on and subpoenas and attacks on the Arab and Muslim community throughout the United States to an extreme. Now we're seeing this effort against solidarity activists with the raids and subpoenas. During the month of October there were grand juries that are being convened, and it remains to be seen what happens, and whether or not this is going to expand, and also what the origin and the breadth of this initial effort is. Obviously, there were attacks like this on the solidarity movement in the '80s with, for example, the attacks against CESPES [Committee in Solidarity with the People of El Salvador].

I think the people are trying to get a good assessment of what's going on. I think it is outrageous, I think it is baseless for the government to be coming in and targeting people engaged in solidarity work. I think it's also reflective of the huge security apparatus that was put in place in the U.S. under Bush and is being accelerated under Obama. I think Obama has responsibility and his Justice Department has responsibility for the fact that they have not made one effort in the time that they've been in office to try and step back from the Bush-era security apparatus. They're not going to, and we didn't think that they would.

SMITH: Well, Mara, you anticipated my next question. I didn't think they would either. But what do you say to a young person who got politically active, say, for the first time in Pennsylvania or Ohio getting people out to vote for Obama, getting on the website of MoveOn, sending money in to Obama, thinking that the pendulum is going to swing back now from where it was under Bush and Cheney and Ashcroft to a better place, and this hasn't happened. How do you explain in a more profound way to people why this hasn't happened, why you thought it would not happen, and where you're coming from?

VERHEYDEN-HILLIARD: Well, we didn't think that there would be a major shift in some of these key issues. I think, in fact, we talked about that on this show around the time Obama was taking office, which was really going to be a question of whether or not the Obama administration was going to expend political capital on these issues when it's not the core of their political belief anyway, to be in opposition to the security state, and, in fact, they have not been. They have ramped it up, and they are clearly not going to be making any efforts, either in ongoing litigation or just in general day-to-day policy efforts, to step back or alter that.

I think the issue for people that came out, that were engaged, that were so enthusiastic and so hopeful for that administration, is that those beliefs, that hope, that thought that you can change the direction of the country that you live in, is absolutely true. It is 100 percent absolutely true. All you need to do is look at the history of the United States for the past one hundred years, hundred fifty years. You look at the struggles over and over again where, at a point in time, people would've thought slavery could not end, people would've thought women would not get the right to vote, you would have thought you would not have been able to get an eight-hour day, that there would be trade unions, that the civil rights struggles, all of those things have happened because people were in the streets. Because people cared, because they came out, because they mobilized, because they had energy.

Every single person that was out there working for Obama or signing up on MoveOn for the Democratic party, should really go back to the core of what sent them out to begin with and think about finding the groups and the organizations that actually are in the streets to make change and recognize it.

It's no fault to hope and to think that an elected official is going to do it, but historically an elected official has never been the one to do it. Elected officials act, to the extent they act, when they feel that there is nearly a revolution coming. If you think about 1964–1965, the Civil Rights Act, the Voting Rights Act, the Congress that passed that was the same Dixiecrat Congress that was in existence ten years earlier, so the politicians hadn't changed. What had changed was the mood of the country and the feeling of the people in the streets.

BOGHOSIAN: I was heartened to see, Mara, in response to the recent raids, that there were a lot of grassroots mobilizations, a lot of rallies. People don't seem to be taking this sitting down.

VERHEYDEN-HILLIARD: Whenever the government does something like this, obviously, it has an impact and it causes a wake and people have a reaction, but the important reaction is to stand up to it. The important reaction is for people to come together and stand in solidarity and to find that right balance. You don't want to be so over the top that there's a hysterical element to things, because you don't really know the scope of anything and you've got to be able to assess what's going on; but you have to take seriously what's happened.

It's a huge burden on the people that are under attack, it ties them up in litigation, it puts your liberty interests at stake. At the same time, people have to be able to recognize what something is, and that the government is in the service of the people. If the government is going to take action like this, the people can get together and stand up and fight back against them.

BOGHOSIAN: You've had so many really tremendous successes in the area of First Amendment rights. What, of all your cases, stands out as the one you're most proud of?

VERHEYDEN-HILLIARD: That's really hard to say, and I think it's because we look at things cumulatively, in a way. Again, going back to the idea that it's not a particular ruling or a particular moment, it's the aggregate impact. That when we look at the past ten years in D.C., the reality was that there was a period of years here, in 2000–2004, when, if you came to Washington for certain demonstrations and militant political activity, lawful, peaceful, but vibrant political activity in the streets, you were at real risk. That by merely coming out and engaging in lawful activities, you were going to end up in a trap-and-detain situation, yanked off the street and thrown in detention. That is no longer the case.

Along with these other tactics, there was the issue of the brutality that was going on. We were stunned to find in the course of our litigation that use of force-reporting requirements had been quietly suspended by the chief of police in the context of mass demonstrations, which basically was telling the cops, "You have a green light to beat people up, because you don't even have to report it." When we found that out, we were able to change that. We were able to change the training, to change the rules on that, and that's had an impact in terms of the issues of brutality against demonstrators.

But now, too, we look at this in the larger context of police brutality and police misconduct against everyone in D.C., not merely the demonstrators. We know that if the police are doing that here, and they're doing that in high profile cases, we know what they may be doing to every single person that gets attacked by the police in D.C., and so we look at the larger scope, as well.

BOGHOSIAN: Mara, what advice do you have for young lawyers who want to work on behalf of social justice?

VERHEYDEN-HILLIARD: I really want to urge people, and particularly law students and young lawyers who are thinking about doing this kind of work, that the most important thing is to do it. Not to try and worry about external factors like, "Am I getting the highest grades and am I achieving someone else's measure or standard of success?"

The thing is to look out there and see what needs to be done and use the tools at your disposal—the law degree that's at your disposal—to go out there and fight for justice and fight for people, because if you can do it, you will be satisfied, you will have a fantastic career doing that. And for people that are not lawyers or law students that want to fight for social justice—particularly in this issue of the Obama administration—everything in this country, everything in the world changes dynamically. You often don't know the change before it happens, but you can be part of the change that makes it happen.

And after it happens, everyone looks back and says, "Oh, well that makes sense." Before it happens, as you look forward, sometimes it's hard to envision.

The only way it will happen is if you're out there fighting for it, and everyone who has a heart and a conscience can do that.

Mara Verheyden-Hilliard was interviewed on Law and Disorder *on November 24, 2008, by Michael Steven Smith and Heidi Boghosian. This interview has been edited and condensed.*

LEONARD WEINGLASS (1933–2011)

Death is not real when one's life work is done well. Even in death, certain men radiate the light of an aurora.

—José Marti

Len was that rare animal: a '50s radical. He developed his values, critical thinking, and world-view in a time when non-conforming was rare. In 1980, he told a newspaper interviewer in Santa Barbara that "I would classify myself as a radical American. I am anti-capitalist in this sense—I don't believe capitalism is now compatible with democracy." He thought Socialism could be, if given a chance. Len argued that Socialism was still a young phenomenon on the world scene, that another world, a non-capitalist world, was possible.

He saw his legal work as his contribution to the collective work of the movement. He didn't care a bit about making a fee. "I want to spend my time defending people who have committed their time to progressive change. That's the criteria. Now, that could be people in armed struggle, people in protest politics, people in confrontational politics, people in mass organizations, people in labor." Defending people against "the machinery of the state," as he put it, was his calling. He felt that one may have a fulfilled and satisfying life if one "aligns with the major thrust of forces in the time in which you live."

The third of four children, he grew up in a Jewish community of two hundred families in Belleville, New Jersey, and attended high school in nearby Kearny, where he was a star on the football team and vice president of his high school class. He played saxophone, was tall and handsome, and sported a '50s pompadour hairstyle, spending a lot of grooming time behind a closed door and in front of the bathroom mirror. His father jokingly complained that he had raised a girl.

When Len graduated, he wanted to take a trip across the country to California. He got his father to drive him to the highway. His dad sat in his car weeping as Len hoisted his thumb at passing trucks. Soon an eighteen-wheeler stopped and Len piled in. He called often from the road, reporting that he was frequently picked up by cars and trucks, that everyone was nice to him, buying him meals and that he was making good time on his trip west.

He didn't take any identification with him. There was a lot of anti-Semitism in the United States in the early '50s. Len didn't want people seeing his last name was Weinglass and identifying him as a Jew. When he got to California he got work on a truck farm, doing stoop farm labor with Japanese agricultural workers. One night, one of them was killed. Len was afraid that without an ID he would be a suspect. He jumped the fence in the middle of the night and got out of there.

He went on to George Washington University in D.C. for college on a scholarship. Len was an outstanding student and was accepted in 1955 into Yale Law School.

Len went from Yale in 1958 directly into the air force. In those days, because of the draft, there was no choice; one had to go into the military. Len was a lawyer in the Judge Advocate General's Corp and rose from second lieutenant to the rank of captain. The air force had charged a black airman with some sort of crime. Len was assigned the case and got him acquitted. This infuriated the brass, which was used to exerting its command influence over the results of military trials.

He was discharged from the air force in 1961 and went on to set up a one-man law practice in Newark, New Jersey. When interviewed by the *New York Times* for Len's obituary, Len's friend and law colleague Michael Krinsky (Len was counsel to the New York firm Rabinowitz, Boudin, Standard, Krinsky &

Lieberman) said he first met Len in Newark in 1969. He considered him "a modern-day Clarence Darrow."

Krinsky told the reporter that Newark "was a rough place to be. A police department and a city administration that was racist and as terrifying as any in America, and there was Lenny representing civil rights people, political people, ordinary people who got charged with stuff and got beat up by the cops. He did it without fame or fortune, and that's what he kept doing, in one way or another." He did it for fifty-three years, being admitted to the bars in New Jersey, California, and New York.

We all know of Len for his famous legal work in the Chicago Seven case with Abbie Hoffman, Dave Dellinger, and Tom Hayden during the Vietnam War period. We remember his expertise in advocating for death-row inmate Mumia Abu-Jamal. He finally got his friend Kathy Boudin out of prison after twenty-three years. He represented Puerto Rican *independentista* Juan Segarra for fifteen years. In the Palestine Eight case, where the defendants were charged with aiding the Marxist Popular Front for the Liberation of Palestine, he was part of a team that stopped their deportation. That took twenty years. David Cole, his co-counsel along with Marc Van der Hout, remembers that Len "coined the term 'terrorologist' while cross-examining the government's expert witness on the Palestine Liberation Organization. He was a joy to work with in the courtroom. Whenever there was a proceeding, our immigration judge, who was Lenny's age, always eagerly wanted to know whether 'Mr. Weinglass' would be appearing."

Len took the tough political cases, the seemingly impossible ones where his clients were charged with heavy crimes like kidnapping, espionage, and murder. "He wasn't drawn to making money. He was drawn to defending justice," Daniel Ellsberg said. "He felt in many cases he was representing one person standing against the state. He was on the side of the underdog. He was also very shrewd in his judgment of juries." Len said that a typical phone call he received started out with the caller saying, "'You're the fifth lawyer I've spoken to.' Then I get interested."

The Cuban Five was Len's last major case. He worked on it for years up to the time of his passing, even reading a court submission from his bed in Montefiore Hospital in the Bronx. The case highlighted what Len considered the U.S. government's hypocrisy in its "war against terror."

Len came into the matter at the appellate level after the Five had been convicted by a prejudiced jury in Miami. His client, Antonio Guerrero and the others, were found guilty of conspiracy to commit espionage against the United States sometime in the future. They were sent from Cuba to Miami by the government of Cuba to spy, not on the United States, but on the counter-revolutionary Cubans in Miami who were launching terrorist activities from Florida directed at persons and property in Cuba, attempting to sabotage the Cuban tourist economy. They gathered information on the Miami-based terrorists, compiling a lengthy dossier on their murderous activities, and turned it over to the FBI. They asked the U.S. government to stop the terrorists, who were targeting the Cuban tourist industry by planting bombs at the Havana airport, on buses, and in a hotel, killing an Italian vacationer. But instead of stopping the terrorists, the U.S. government used the dossier to figure out the identities of the Cuban Five, had them arrested, prosecuted, convicted, and sentenced to long prison terms.

What Len said about the use of the conspiracy charge is illustrative of his precision and clarity of thought. Conspiracy has always been the charge used by the prosecution in political cases. A conspiracy is an agreement between people to commit a substantive crime. By using the charge of conspiracy, the government is relieved of the requirement that the underlying crime be proven. All the government has to prove to a jury is that there was an agreement to do the crime. The individuals charged with conspiracy are convicted even if the underlying crime was never committed. In the case of the Five, the Miami jury was asked to find that there was an agreement to commit espionage. The government never had to prove that espionage actually happened. It could not have proven that espionage occurred. None of the Five sought or possessed any top-secret information or U.S. national defense secrets.

Len had an ironic and wry sense of humor. He had a large one-room cabin atop a high hill overlooking the Rondout Reservoir in New York's Catskill Mountains. He lived in a teepee there off and on for several years before designing the cottage. He had a special joy, which he inherited from his mother, Clara, for gardening and raising fruit trees. This was an especially difficult pursuit because he had mistakenly planted the trees on the south side of the hill where they got plenty of sun but were vulnerable to a false spring, blooming early, then getting damaged by a frost, which could occur up there as late as June. Nonetheless Len persisted and sometimes got a crop of apples, pears, and plums. The crop would then be eaten by the neighborhood bears. "I grow the fruit," Len complained, "then the bears come and eat it and I go to Gristedes."

He kept his sense of humor even during those terrible final days at Montefiore Hospital. His surgeon operated on him but abandoned his attempt to remove what turned out to be a large spreading malignant tumor, undetected by the pre-op CT-scan. When the surgeon saw what it really was, that it was an inoperable tumor, he could do nothing but sew Len back up and tell him the bad news. Len looked up at us from his bed in the recovery room alter being informed by the surgeon, and said, simply, "summary judgment." And so it was. He lived but another six weeks, steadily declining, never getting to go home, never giving up, even as several doctors told him "you are in the final stretch."

Len was strong and vigorous up to his last illness. Since his high school days he never lost his interest in football, and closely followed the professional game. He was a Giants fan, of course, but sentimentally he liked the Green Bay Packers because they were the only team in the league owned not by billionaires but by the municipality of Green Bay. While Len was in Montefiore Hospital the Packers made it into the Super Bowl against the Pittsburgh Steelers. "Want to bet on the game?" I asked. "How about five bucks." He raised his finger to the sky. "Ten?" I ventured. "No," he whispered, "fifty." So my nephew Ben got us a bookie in Connecticut and we put down fifty bucks apiece. The Packers were favored so we had to give away three and a half points. Len advised that this was a responsible bet. It sure was. The Packers wound up winning in the last quarter by four points. I congratulated Len on his sagacity. That win lifted his spirits.

Len was a longtime member of the National Lawyers Guild and served for a time as the co-chair of its international committee. He was the recipient of the Guild's Ernie Goodman Award, named after the extraordinary Detroit Socialist lawyer and Guild leader who helped build the auto workers union and later organized the Guild to send its members down south to protect black people during the civil rights movement.

The Dean of Yale Law School, Robert C. Post, wrote Len's sister, Elaine, to express his sympathy, writing that "Leonard Weinglass lived a full and admirable life in the law and exemplified the spirit of citizenship that lawyers at their very best display. He brought great honor to the legal community and to Yale Law School, which takes pride in all he did and was."

Len was a Jew, but rejected the idea that it was racial ties or bonds of blood that made up the Jewish community, seeing that view as a degenerate philosophy leading to chauvinism and cruelty. He rejected Jewish nationalism, embracing instead an unconditional solidarity with the persecuted and exterminated.

Len was not religious. The emergency room admitting nurse asked him what his religion was so she could fill out the questionnaire. He paused and answered, "Leave it blank." Two weeks later, when he was admitted to the hospital, he again was asked what his religion was. "None," he answered.

Len died the evening of March 23, 2011, as spring was approaching in New York. He had plans to celebrate Passover in April, as usual, with his family in New Jersey. He knew quite a lot about Passover, led his family's observance at the Seder every year, and kept up a file on the holiday. He liked the idea that the Jews had the chutzpah to conflate their own flight from slavery with spring and the liberation of nature.

He had plans to tend his fruit trees on the side of the hill next to his Catskill cabin. He would have put in a vegetable garden near his three-block-long driveway, which frequently washed out and which he repaired with Sisyphean regularity. He would have set out birdseed on the cabin's porch rail, where he would sit in a lounge chair on a platform and watch the songbirds feed.

He loved being out on that porch, high up on a hill, particularly at day's end, seeing the sun go down over the Rondout Reservoir, which supplies some of the drinking water to New York City. Back in 1976, he told a student reporter for UCLA's *Daily Bruin* that leading a committed life was satisfying, fulfilling, and made him happy.

He will be remembered personally as a good, generous, and loyal friend, a gentle and kind person; politically as a great persuasive speaker, an acute analyst of the political scene, and a far-seeing visionary. Professionally, Len Weinglass will live on as one of the great lawyers of his time, joining the legal pantheon of leading twentieth-century advocates for justice along with Clarence Darrow, Leonard Boudin, Arthur Kinoy, Ernest Goodman, and William Kunstler.

"Lenny cannot be replaced," wrote his friend Sandra Levinson. "There are no words for the loss we all feel. Do something brave, put yourself out there for someone, fight for someone's dignity, do something to honor this courageous, just man."

Leonard Irving Weinglass: *Presente!*

BILL SCHAAP

William H. Schaap, radical lawyer and co-founder/publisher of CovertAction Quarterly and Sheridan Square Press, died on February 25, 2016, of pulmonary disease at his apartment in Manhattan. He was seventy-five.

Born in Brooklyn, New York on March 1, 1940, to Maurice and Leah (née Lerner) Schaap, Bill Schaap was raised in Freeport, New York. His older brother was the late sports broadcaster and author Dick Schaap. Bill received his BA from Cornell University in 1961. He graduated in 1964 from the law school of the University of Chicago, where he became part of the civil rights movement in 1963, counseling students arrested for protesting segregated housing.

After receiving his law degree, he worked as an associate for several years at the Wall Street firm of Fried, Frank, Harris, Shriver & Jacobson. During this time, he joined the radical National Lawyers Guild, and his commitment to civil rights, opposition to the Vietnam War, and leftist political causes deepened. In 1968, when Columbia students were arrested for occupying a building on campus, Schaap represented and got many of them released from jail.

When William Kunstler, president of the Center for Constitutional Rights, asked Schaap to head a project to defend U.S. military resisters to the Vietnam War, Schaap left his Wall Street law firm. He and his wife, Ellen Ray, spent three years in Japan and Germany counseling and defending American GI resisters. Though he had no previous training in military law, he learned on the job and stated that he never lost a single case.

Schaap was an articulate and relentless opponent of the Vietnam War. In the early '70s, he and Ray were arrested along with several others for protesting the war at a session of Congress. From the visitors' gallery they interrupted the proceedings by playing tapes of the U.S. bombing of Vietnam.

Schaap and Ray moved in 1976 to Washington, D.C., where he became the editor of the Military Law Reporter. *With Louis Wolf and the controversial former CIA operative Philip Agee, Schaap and Ray founded and edited* CovertAction Information Bulletin, *which eventually expanded into a glossy, source-noted magazine* called *CovertAction Quarterly. Initially, the focus of the magazine was the illegal activities of the CIA around the world, but it later branched out to report on domestic abuses by the National Security Agency and FBI.*

In 1980, Schaap and Ray moved to New York City and founded Sheridan Square Press, first publishing books about the CIA by former CIA agents and later a wider variety of books. When President Ronald Reagan's former national security adviser, Robert McFarlane, sued Sheridan Square Press for libeling him in Ari Ben-Menashe's book Profits of War, *Sheridan Square lost its financial backers and was forced to shut down. The case was eventually thrown out by the courts.*

In 1986, Schaap and Ray founded the non-profit Institute for Media Analysis and began publishing Lies of Our Times, *a magazine of media criticism that analyzed the underlying political assumptions and biases of the* New York Times *and other mainstream media.*

Ellen Ray, Schaap's wife and work partner of forty-five years, died of lymphoma in June 2015.

MICHAEL STEVEN SMITH: I was a subscriber to *CovertAction Quarterly*, as was Michael Ratner. A great magazine. What was the purpose of the magazine? After so many years doing legal work you now had on a journalist/editor hat; what did you try to accomplish with the magazine?

BILL SCHAAP: We started it on a shoestring, and the original purpose was just to expose the CIA. We worked with Lou Wulf, who was an expert at uncovering CIA agents at U.S. embassies, not through any classified documents; but because if you knew how to read the paperwork and State Department stuff, you could tell who the ringers were, and you knew these people were CIA. And we were so successful that Congress passed a law against us.

SMITH: The magazine *CovertAction* was really famous and well known. It was doing the highest level of American journalism. And for a number of years, there were actually lists of CIA people who were disrupting the politics of other countries that you guys published. So, talk about that for a minute.

SCHAAP: Our goal was to try and make these people ineffective, because the only way most CIA case officers could work, particularly the ones that were assigned to an embassy, was to pretend to be something else. They were all third assistant political secretaries, second assistant, whatever. And those were all phony things. Their job was to inveigle their way into various community organizations in whatever foreign capital they might have been posted, to recruit people to turn against their own countries, be traitors to their own countries, and become spies for the U.S. We thought that if we identified these people beforehand, it might make their job a little harder, which it did.

Of course, the problem was that the government said we were trying to get them killed, which we weren't trying to do, and nobody we exposed ever did get killed. But they were very fortunate in that one CIA station chief in Athens, named Richard Welch, was exposed by a Greek group and assassinated. So for a long time, everybody, including President Gerald Ford, tried to say that he got assassinated because we'd exposed him. And, in fact, we hadn't. Later, with the help of Mort Halperin, who had connections to the State Department, we discovered cables where Welch had been warned not to move into his predecessor's house in Athens, because everybody in Athens knew that was where the CIA station chief lived, and we found a cable he sent back, saying, "I'm sorry, my wife really likes the house. We're going to move in." And they moved in, and about three days later he was gunned down on the front steps.

SMITH: There's someone you haven't mentioned yet, Phil Agee. He's dead now, but he published a book called *Inside the Company,* which exposed the names of hundreds of agents subverting democracy and unionization in Latin America, Central America. Now, he had some relationship to the magazine.

SCHAAP: We founded it with him. He had been an adviser to *CounterSpy. CounterSpy,* which folded when Welch got killed, because the pressure was too much. So we started a new one called *CovertAction,* and we worked with Phil directly the whole time. He was not the person who was discovering who the undercover people were; Lou Wulf was doing that. But Phil wrote articles for us in every issue, and we worked very closely with him. And in fact, some of us traveled around the world when he was asked to go to various places to try to expose CIA operations. The most well-known was Jamaica, when the CIA was trying to overthrow the government of Michael Manley. The government asked Phil Agee to come down and help, and Phil asked Ellen Ray to come down and help him help them. Once you start exposing these things, they really don't have any defense.

HEIDI BOGHOSIAN: Were you harassed yourself? And was *CovertAction* infiltrated or attempts made to close the magazine down?

SCHAAP: So far as we know, we weren't infiltrated, because it was just the three of us. I mean, we waxed the galleys, we rolled them down, we did everything. So, they couldn't actually infiltrate the organization. But they certainly did try to catch us in something phony. We would get tips that turned out to be CIA trying to get us to print some story that wasn't true so they could then discredit us. No, we actually had more direct interference from the government when we were doing the military law work before *CovertAction.* The military is always a bit more heavy-handed than the CIA, and they would plant bugs in our attic, things like that.

But they didn't know we were very close to a lot of MPs, and they used to bring us the transcripts and show us that they were recording everything that was going on at the legal counseling. I ended up getting one hundred court-martial convictions thrown out because they were eavesdropping on the defense attorney. And if you proved the defense attorney was being eavesdropped, you won the case.

SMITH: After you published the names of CIA agents for many years, they passed a law. You would have to call it the *CovertAction Information Bulletin* Law, because it was passed to stop your work, which was all taken from public sources. Tell us about that law and what's been its history as we've gone forward.

SCHAAP: It's only been used a few times. It's called the Intelligence Identities Protection Act (1982), and there are two parts. One makes it a crime for someone in the government who has classified information to reveal someone's identity. But the second part makes it a crime to reveal the identity of someone you did not learn from classified information or from your position, *if*—and this was the tricky part—*if* you were in the business of exposing these kinds of people. At one point, Floyd Abrams had gone down to Washington on behalf of the AP, CBS, and the *New York Times* to protest the law. And then he came back and he said, "Nobody has to worry. They're only interested in getting *CovertAction Magazine*." And I said, "Thanks a lot, Floyd."

MICHAEL RATNER: I want to address that for a second, because it's a really interesting point. What happened is the argument that was made was that if you used these names in a legitimate way, like you're exposing one agent who may have eavesdropped on somebody or murdered somebody, then a newspaper could do that. But if it was the business, quote "the business or the work of the magazine to expose agents in general," although there was always a purpose for *CovertAction* doing it, then it violated the law. And they sold that to the Congress and they passed that law.

But what the effect has been as I see it, is that even magazines that are only going to publish one name about what an agent's doing in Haiti, or somewhere else, are completely nervous about it and don't do it.

The laws had what we lawyers call a chilling effect—so magazines don't actually publish the names. And now they're developing a shield law for journalists, and there's what they call an "Assange Exception." It's going to protect journalists as long as the journal or the publisher doesn't have as its main business publishing classified or confidential documents.

SCHAAP: Right. That's the same idea.

RATNER: It won't protect people like WikiLeaks, but it will protect the *New York Times.* It's as if, somehow, there are legitimate publishers and illegitimate publishers.

SCHAAP: Yeah, and they and a judge get to decide which is which, according to their policy.

RATNER: What happens is, no one takes a risk after that.

SCHAAP: Yes, it's very, very rare. I mean, you will see it on occasion—the whole thing with Valerie Plame.

RATNER: Right. Only after that was all over the place. I mean, in the beginning, even the *New York Times* and other papers wouldn't say the name of this person. But once that person's name was in one hundred magazines and ten television shows, they started naming it. But the law itself has only been used once or twice. Once was in the Plame case and another case, which is very not well known, was a Bill Kunstler case, of a Native American Marine embassy guard who had told somebody—who turned out to be a Russian spy—who a couple of the CIA people at that particular embassy were. And it's a very hard case to find, because it was a court-martial, it wasn't a federal court case. And the charge against him in the court-martial was violating the Intelligence Identities Protection Law. But those, as far as we know, are the only two times it's ever been used.

SCHAAP: Right, but the reason it's been used so rarely is because no one's publishing the names of CIA agents anymore.

SMITH: Bill, you published a book long before I ever met you, a book that I bought and read and cherished, about Jim Garrison, the district attorney in New Orleans who investigated the Kennedy assassination. Tell us what was behind that, because it was quite an extraordinary thing when you published that book.

SCHAAP: We got a call from Mary Howell, the Guild lawyer in New Orleans. She was a friend of Jim Garrison's, and she said Jim had a manuscript but his publisher had rejected it. They thought it was a little too outré. We went down to meet with him and Ellen said, "Oh, Jim Garrison, my idol. I'm in love." The problem was, he had written the book in the third person, and it was obvious that the book should be written in the first person.

We hired Zach Sklar, who was a great editor at the time. We re-did the book, and it became *JFK* and it was a best seller. Later, at a film festival in Havana, we met Oliver Stone. And Ellen said to him, "Have I got a property for you!" Because we knew he was an assassination freak, we gave him an advance copy of the book. That same night, he called and said, "It's really very interesting. I can't do anything with it, but it's really very interesting." And the next day he called and said, "Listen, it's really very interesting. Don't sell it to anybody else." Then the third day, he called and said, "I want to buy it, but you have to keep it top secret until I do the film." Which we did, and he made a hell of a film.

Of course, Oliver Stone won't admit to any of this!

SMITH: You published a newsletter called *Lies of Our Times,* and it was aimed at the newspaper that prints everything that's fit, the *New York Times.* But more generally, it was devised to expose government disinformation and propaganda.

SCHAAP: It was in the '90s, from 1990 to 1995, I think. We did six years of it. To a certain extent, the abuses we were crying about got a little bit less over time, because that sometimes is the helpful result of this kind of exposure. But we were just tired with people thinking that if it was in the *New York Times,* it must be true. Or, if Dan Rather said it, it must be true. And the fact is, those people lie all the time if it suits their people's needs. So, we had a great run. Noam Chomsky did a regular column every issue for us and we had a lot of really good writers from all over the world, mostly from the States explaining how stories that had become gospel were really completely untrue.

BOGHOSIAN: Bill, you've taught courses on propaganda and disinformation at John Jay College of Criminal Justice and you've been in the field for decades. How do you comment on the American people's response to recent revelations of the ubiquitous surveillance state and a secret government? Have things changed for the better or the worse in terms of public awareness and response?

SCHAAP: I think they've changed a bit for the better. We're still way behind Europe, where the average European is skeptical of anything its government says. That's not so much the case here, but I think we've gotten to a point where people recognize that the government lies to them. They recognize that there's an awful lot that goes on that they don't know very much about. It's a big step up from the '60s and '70s, when most Americans had no idea. They didn't know what the NSA was. The NSA was secret. They barely knew what the CIA was. And they had no idea that all that stuff was going on, nor did they have any notion of the degree to which the government had influence in the media, particularly the foreign media. One of the CIA's best operations was to control journalists all over the world, including American journalists. But sometimes you didn't even have to, because you could plant a story with an agent in Germany, and then Reuters would pick it up and then AP would pick it up, and then the story that the CIA guy wrote would be on the front page of the American papers without anybody publishing it being aware of that.

BOGHOSIAN: I wanted to ask Bill what advice you would have for young attorneys considering a progressive practice who may be frightened by government tactics?

SCHAAP: The fact of the matter is that, as we know from Lawyers Guild people all over the country, you can be a politically active, politically conscious lawyer and still make a living. You're not going to be a Wall Street tycoon, but there is a large chunk of the American people who are progressive, and most of them, when they have legal stuff, they'd rather have a progressive lawyer. It doesn't mean you have to defend them against some big criminal case. I mean, progressive people want a progressive lawyer to do their will or buy their house or do their whatever. I don't necessarily encourage progressives to become lawyers, but I do encourage lawyers to become progressives.

"Remembering Attorney Bill Schaap" appeared, in slightly different form, on Law and Disorder *on February 29, 2016.*

Bill Schaap was interviewed on Law and Disorder *on August 7, 2015, by Michael Steven Smith, Michael Ratner, and Heidi Boghosian. This interview has been edited and condensed.*

RHONDA COPELON

The progressive feminist lawyer Rhonda Copelon (1945–2010) was a professor at CUNY School of Law for twenty-six years. She was a staff attorney and then vice president at the Center for Constitutional Rights, where she broke new ground opening U.S. federal courts and international tribunals to gender-based violence and international human rights violations.

With co-counsel Peter Weiss, she won the landmark human rights case Filártiga v. Peña-Irala, *which established that victims of gross human rights abuses committed abroad had recourse to U.S. courts and paved the way for universal jurisdiction. She argued the* Harris v. McRae *case before the U.S. Supreme Court, losing when the court upheld the Hyde Amendment, which prohibited Medicaid reimbursement for almost all abortions poor women sought.*

Losing *Harris v. McRae*

MICHAEL STEVEN SMITH: Rhonda Copelon argued the *McRae* case [*Harris v. McRae* (1980)] in the Supreme Court, which tried to get the federal government to pay for poor women's abortions. Unfortunately, Rhonda, the court rejected your arguments. Still today, we have a situation where poor women who seek abortions cannot get federal funding.

RHONDA COPELON: Let me say first that I would state it differently, Michael. We didn't go to court to get Medicaid for women. We went to court to save it. Because the reality between 1970, when we began to have liberalized abortion laws, and 1976, was that most states funded Medicaid. The reason I think that's important is that *McRae* has become a two-line footnote in textbooks today. There is a certain way in which people have just accepted that Medicaid doesn't have to pay for abortions.

The more these terrible precedents come down, the more people absorb them as culture, as opposed to as bad and as needing to be reversed.

I would also want to put this case in a larger political perspective. I think there are a couple of things that are relevant to today. One is that historically, based on race and class, women have been treated differently in terms of their reproductive rights. Anti-abortion laws in the United States first came about as a way to be sure that the WASP population, the white population of the U.S., would not be out-reproduced by the immigrant population. The way to do that was to cut back on abortion.

It was also to get rid of women lay healers. Abortion was a very central part of the healers' work. Because of that, they also became, in a sense, the doctors for women. The doctors were working to become professional in the mid-nineteenth century. They had to get rid of this. If you made abortion criminal, then you took away this very significant connection between women needing medical care and women providing it. There was a little bit of "human life" stuff even then, but it wasn't significant, and the [Catholic] Church didn't think it was significant until 1875. The point is that even our original abortion laws were class-based.

Then you come into the early twentieth century, and you have class-based eugenics laws. You have *Buck v. Bell* [1927] and you have class-based sterilization laws, which said you sterilize those who are socially inappropriate. That was a very broad category. The fact that that was still going on in the '70s was rediscovered when it was realized that poor women who were on welfare were being told that they would lose their welfare if they bore another child.

Then along comes abortion as a right.

SMITH: But under the case you lost, *McRae*, it's the opposite. Because that's depriving poor women of abortions. You would think if they were worried about being outnumbered by poor people or minorities that they would say, "Have all the abortions you want. In fact, we'll pay for them and we'll give you a house if you do it."

COPELON: You've got it. What is it that twisted that history in ways that seem irrational? I think the basic thing that did that was religion; the religious opposition to abortion. The Catholic Church issued in the mid-'70s a pastoral plan for pro-life activities. They said their goal was a human life amendment, which meant a complete prohibition on abortion. They had to take it little by little. The first little, of course, is who? The most powerless. The poor women who are dependent on "taxpayer money."

What you get is this immense mobilization to stop Medicaid funding for poor women for abortions. It was a fundamentally religious mobilization. All of the literature was religious. The debates in Congress were religious. It was supported, as were many candidates and other laws that were being passed, within the churches on Sundays. The money for the New York State Right to Life Committee came from the coffers on Sundays.

Then in 1978, you had a historic coming together, which had never happened before in this country in the same way, of the Catholic Church and the Protestant Evangelicals. They came together on the issue of abortion.

That gave the other side a political power that they've never had. That is the Republican Party today. That is the federal judiciary. If we don't win back the Supreme Court in a solid way, which we don't even have now on *Roe v. Wade*, we are dead in the water for many, many more years than we think.

I think it's very important to look at the role of extremist religion in this country. When you look at the megachurches, you see the power that they've had to undo the First Amendment in terms of the establishment of religion to gain all kinds of economic advantages.

The Hyde Amendment was the cutoff of Medicaid. In the *McRae* case we were challenging this on the ground that it was a violation of the separation of church and state because it was based on a fundamentally religious idea, and because the support in the society was fundamentally religious. It seems we were at the cusp of something that has grown into an even greater monster.

Winning *Filártiga v. Peña-Irala*

COPELON: *Filártiga* opened the federal courts to claims based on human rights under a statute called the Alien Tort Claims Act, which provided a basis for non-citizens to bring actions in federal court: tort actions, actions for wrongs that violated the treaties of the United States—or what is called customary international law, which is international norms that are widely adopted as obligatory and often as absolute.

When we started that case, there had been no human rights cases that had been successful under the Alien Tort Claims Act. It was a statute that was passed in 1789 with the original Judiciary Act. It had lain fallow for a very long time, and only used in a couple of instances which were more commercial than human rights-oriented.

The plaintiffs were Dr. Joel Filártiga and Dolly Filártiga, both Paraguayans. Dr. Filártiga was a leading dissident against the [Alfredo] Stroessner regime, one of the most brutal and long-lasting in all of Latin America. As a doctor, he ran a couple of clinics. One was in the countryside for the *campesinos*, and one was in Asunción, where the family lived.

His son, Joelito, was taken one night by the Paraguayan police to the station. He was tortured. He died in the course of the torture, which I don't think they intended. They intended to torture him to punish Dr. Filártiga. They dragged him over to a neighbor's house and tried to make it look as if it was a killing in a heat of passion by the neighbor's lover.

Peña-Irala, who was the police official, called Dr. Filártiga's sister, Dolly, to come get his body. She didn't know she was getting his body. She came and dragged the body back to her house. Peña-Irala told her: "Now you have what you've been looking for."

The Filártiga family was amazingly courageous. They did what Emmett Till's mother did. They put Dr. Filártiga's tortured body on the table in the house and thousands of people walked in to witness it. This in the middle of one of the most brutal dictatorships.

They brought a case in the local court and they were surrounded at night by police who were clicking their rifles all night long. They slept under their beds. There was a continuing trauma. Their lawyer was arrested. Dolly and her mother spent several nights in jail.

Then one day a letter arrives. It is delivered to the Filártiga household by someone who worked for a U.S. corporation. The letter has the return address of Peña. They steamed it open and they found that Peña was living in Flushing, New York. They re-steamed it back. Peña's Paraguayan residence was only a few doors away. That's one of the horrible ironies here. They brought it back to him.

Dolly said to her father, "I'm going to New York. We need to have justice." She had a sense of needing justice. She didn't know what that would be, but she just wanted justice. She convinced him. At first, he was reluctant, and then he came with her. They got the Paraguayan community mobilized here. They found him [Peña] selling hotdogs in Flushing Meadows. He was arrested by the Immigration and Naturalization Service [INS]. He was in the Brooklyn Navy Yard.

First, Peter [Weiss] got a call from Amnesty International saying, "There's a Paraguayan torturer in the Brooklyn Navy Yard. Is there anything we can do?" Then Peter called me and I said, "Well, you know, Peter, years ago you were looking at this old statute that you were thinking of, that various people were thinking of using. The Allende family in Chile was thinking of using it for the U.S. involvement in the coup and the murder of Allende. The My Lai victims were thinking of using it. So maybe this is something we should look at."

We looked at it and it said an alien has a claim for tort only in violation of the law of nations. I didn't know very much about the law of nations at the time, but Peter was our resident brilliant international expert, who we all thought was in the clouds, until this happened.

He said, "Well, torture is a violation of international law." I said, "Okay, so then why can't we do this case? We should do this case." There was actually a dispute at the Center for Constitutional Rights (CCR) because people thought we'd lost it. We are noted for doing things that other people think shouldn't be done. We finally convinced everybody that we should do it.

Dolly came up with her wonderful lawyer, Michael Maggio. She was seeking asylum. We prepared a complaint, which we filed the next day. There was no time to worry over how beautiful and adequate this complaint was. It was served on Peña in the Brooklyn Navy Yard.

Then we had to try and stop him from being moved out. We went to the court and the court was a little reluctant. "I really can't tell the immigration people what to do." It was the Carter administration and so we called the head of immigration and we said, "You know, we're worried he's on a fast track, even though most people were not, and we want you to keep him here." They actually never moved him out. We went to the Supreme Court to get him to stay. They couldn't give it to us, but they actually kept him. They kept him here.

In the District Court, the judge said, "I agree that prohibition of torture is probably becoming a norm of international law, but all the prior decisions are against me, so I can't rule in your favor." At that point, he was sent home and we appealed.

Peña got a new lawyer, who was a much better lawyer, and they made it a much more complicated case of what we call federal jurisdiction. What right did Congress have to even pass this law when it came to the federal courts? Was it just overreaching by Congress, with us having no business being there? It was a much more sophisticated argument as we got further up.

We were told we were out of our minds. Every time I've gone into court, even more recently on a Filártiga-type case, the judge says, "Why is a case involving," for example, "a person from Algeria, a perpetrator from Algeria, a victim from Algeria, that occurred in Algeria, what's it doing here?" Same thing about Paraguay, about anywhere, because they couldn't understand how they could have jurisdiction over something that really didn't have these points of contact with the United States. Well, the contact is that he's here. You can sue a person when they come here. That's been very important to the whole line of cases that CCR has developed since *Filártiga*.

At any rate, the court had as the presiding judge Irving Kaufman. Kaufman was the judge who sentenced the Rosenbergs to death. Every once in a while in Irving's life, he's tried to do something very great for civil liberties. We don't know if this is expiation or not. I think this was perhaps one of them. But we had a very decent bench.

Kaufman kept saying, "What does the State Department think about this? What does the State Department think about this?" Of course, our argument was that "it doesn't really matter, Judge, what the State Department thinks. You are a court. You're independent of the State Department. You have to act as an independent judiciary." Well, we got back to the office and the clerk called us saying that the court had asked the State Department for an opinion.

SMITH: This was the Jimmy Carter period, so we at least had some hope, plus I think you knew some of the people.

COPELON: Peter knew some of the people who had been there for a long time. What I only learned two years ago from the then, and first, Assistant Secretary for Human Rights, Patt Derian, was that the Latin Americanists in the State Department knew all about wanting an amicus brief and didn't tell her. They tried to keep the Human Rights Bureau out of the subject. She got to know about it because I was called by someone from the Justice Department. They had sent it over to the Justice Department to draft the brief and they wanted our thoughts on it. Peter knew people in the legal adviser's office who are the longer-term folks who are very progressive. All of that conspired against what had been the State Department's view that you support these dictatorships. You don't undermine them. That was very key in terms of the timing of the case.

The U.S. came out with a fantastic amicus brief. Really, it gave us everything we could have possibly wanted. Of course, I don't want to credit Kaufman with courage here, but he delivered a brilliant, ringing opinion saying that torture is a violation of international law and that the Alien Tort Claims Act gives non-citizens a right to bring cases in respect of norms of that dimension in international law.

SMITH: It really opened the door for the cases in the United States, where the CCR and now other institutions have gone on and sued all kinds of dictators, as well as corporations who do this. It's the basis for the Convention Against Torture, for the Pinochet case, for making torture something that could actually be sued on anywhere in the world.

COPELON: It was based, in a sense, on principle. Though we had a statute, it was based on a principle of universal jurisdiction that you can't escape your wrongs by crossing national borders. That actually was an old principle of Anglo-American law that we used very effectively in the argument to say, "We have a principle. It's called transitory tort. Your wrongs stay on your back. You can't get out from under them. If you come here, you're still suable and you're suable in state court."

We said, "You know, Judge, we don't really think you want these cases to go to state court because these are federal cases involving international issues." That was very helpful in moving a court. You move a court by appealing to their sense of power or need, as well as to whatever your rights and norms may be. It was a great victory. I might say it happened on the very same day that we lost *McRae* 5–4. It was June 30, 1980.

SMITH: The same day you lost *McRae* is the day you won *Filártiga*?

COPELON: You'll love this story, Michael.

In the morning, I called the deputy clerk of the Supreme Court. He said, "Are you sitting down?" I said, "Uh oh." He said, "You lost 5–4."

That was *McRae*. I had been pessimistic about winning because I saw the neoliberal tilt of the court, to the idea that the state had no obligation to help you exercise your fundamental rights. *McRae* wasn't the beginning, but it was a very big step in the elaboration of the neoliberal constitution, which was then announced later in a case involving an abused child, by Rehnquist, saying, "Ours is a negative constitution. The state has no obligation to protect you."

SMITH: It was the beginning of the unwinding of the New Deal.

COPELON: Exactly. I was very pessimistic that we could overcome that, even though we brought in all the health issues, all the religious issues. I was pessimistic. I lost that in the morning.

That afternoon—you remember Beth Bachnak who was our education person. She walked in. She was very sensitive. She said, "Rhonda, you will not be able to take this in, but the clerk of the Second Circuit just called." This was about 2:00 p.m. "You won *Filártiga*." I said, "Oh, give me a break." I was on my way to a press conference about *McRae.* I think Peter had a more immediate rush with this victory, but it took me about two months, because I was so pained by the result in *McRae.* That defeat was very life-changing for me, in a way, because it felt like it made privileges a right and showed that there was a real limit on what you could do with the Constitution. Then here comes *Filártiga* saying, "You know, you can actually do human rights." *Filártiga* made me think human rights is where I need to go because human rights has a different approach to economic and social rights. It has a different approach to issues like this than in our Constitution.

I think what happens with bringing human rights in is you have a universal standard that is increasingly being accepted, that the U.S. appears more and more to be an outlaw to. I'm so excited that today there's a U.S. human rights network, that people are actually talking about human rights in a real way, that we have the National Economic and Social Rights Initiative talking about economic and social rights in this country. I think all of that is some of the answer, in a way, to *McRae.*

The CCR built on *Filártiga* through a line of cases. We sued Radovan Karadzic, who was head of the Bosnian Serbs, who has just been arrested by the International Criminal Tribunal for the former Yugoslavia. That case broadened *Filártiga* because Karadzic was a non-state actor. That precedent opened the door to many cases against various dictatorships and their lackeys. The notion of crimes against humanity, and that a private actor could commit crimes against humanity, was then applied to corporations. That led to the Unocal case [2002], which challenged the military abuse of people with Unocal's consent and active involvement during the construction of a pipeline in Burma. The case has very large reach and is very important.

We were terrified a few years ago when the Supreme Court took the issue of whether or not the Alien Tort Claims Act was constitutionally grounded. We made it through that one [6–3]. But we shouldn't be too confident about that, either.

Rhonda Copelon was interviewed on Law and Disorder *on September 29, 2008, by Michael Steven Smith. This interview has been edited and condensed.*

PETER WEISS

New York City attorney Peter Weiss (b. 1925) was part of the leadership of the Center for Constitutional Rights from its early days in the 1960s, serving on its board of directors for nearly fifty years. He helped guide the Center in its international human rights work. He formed and served as president of the Lawyers Committee on Nuclear Policy, and was the chair of the board of the Institute for Policy Studies, a radical think tank in Washington, D.C.

MICHAEL STEVEN SMITH: I know that you came with your parents from Europe, with the bad guys in hot pursuit. Can you tell us a little about your background, and about the significant cases you've been involved in?

PETER WEISS: I was born in Vienna. When the Nazis came in 1938, my parents decided to go to France. We lived there for two and a half years, and then came to the United States in 1941. I attended the Straubenmuller Textile High School (now called Charles Evans Hughes) because my parents decided that the first Jews to be killed would be the intellectuals, so they wanted me to have a trade.

I took a course in power weaving. I got a scholarship from the Ethical Culture Society to go to St. John's College in Annapolis, also known as the "Great Books" college. After two years there, I was drafted into the army. Eventually I wound up in military intelligence, because of my languages, mostly German.

Then I spent a year, after I was demobilized in 1946, working for U.S. military government in its decartelization branch, which was supposed to break up the German cartels. That didn't last very long, because somebody in Washington decided they needed the cartels to fight the commies.

SMITH: By cartels, you mean big corporations like Krupp and Bayer Aspirin?

WEISS: And I. G. Farben. It was a very exciting time. It got me interested in the law. Then I went back and finished St. John's. At the end of that two-year period, I applied to a bunch of law schools, saying that I wanted to work for what was then going to be the International Trade Organization based in Havana, Cuba, which was supposed to break up the cartels worldwide. The admissions people at Yale seemed to like that, so I got into Yale Law School. But I never did anything about cartels again after that.

MICHAEL RATNER: You then became a trademark lawyer, which is your specialty, right? Intellectual property, really. I first knew you when I went to the Center for Constitutional Rights in 1971. I remember you best because, at that time, none of us knew anything about international law. I always tell the story, Peter insisted that we put international law claims into every single piece of litigation we did.

How did you get from Yale to international law, and the importance of human rights in international law?

WEISS: I took an international law course at Yale with one of the great international lawyers of that time, Myres McDougall, former president of the American Society of International Law. He has produced a number of quite progressive international lawyers, like Burns Weston and Richard Falk. But also some conservative ones.

That got me interested in international law, plus my multinational background. Having lived in France and been born in Austria, I somehow, for some reason, believed in international law.

RATNER: What was your end goal, in terms of international law?

WEISS: You guys are all too young to remember that, but the end of the war was a very progressive period in terms of people's expectations. People thought that was the last big war. And now we were going on to build a peaceful, just world. Some talked about world government. I actually spent a few months working for a foundation for world government. Others believed this was going to be the period in history when poverty would be done away with. There was a great deal of interest in economic development then.

I actually spent my first two years after graduating from Yale, in 1952, running an organization called IDPA: the International Development Placement Association, which was a precursor of the Peace Corps. Then at the end of those two years, I had to start making a living, because the Internal Revenue Service decided that sending young Americans to work in what were then called under-developed countries was not entitled to tax exemption. That put the IDPA out of business and I had to go and practice law.

RATNER: What do you consider to be your most significant litigations or legal work?

WEISS: One was the *Filártiga* case that I did at the Center with my colleagues Rhonda Copelon, principally, and John Corwin, which brought the Alien Tort Claims Act back to life in 1978. Another was a case that I worked on in the '90s at the International Court of Justice, obtaining an advisory opinion on the illegality of nuclear weapons.

RATNER: Let's go to the first one, *Filártiga v. Peña-Irala,* which is the Alien Tort Claims statute. I remember being at the Center at the time; this was a case in which there was a torture committed in Paraguay, against a young man who was killed eventually. His family happened to come to the United States, and the man who engaged in the torture eventually came to the United States. That's Peña-Irala.

You decided that somehow, even though everything happened in Paraguay, a court in the United States could actually do something. It became probably the most important human rights case ever brought in the United States.

WEISS: The reason we thought that was because, almost ten years prior, we discovered a very old law, going back to the First Judiciary Act of 1789, which in one sentence said that an alien has a right of action, in an American court, for a tort in violation of the law of nations, which is what they called international law in the eighteenth century.

We lost it in the first instance, even though we had a sympathetic judge. We had Judge Eugene Nickerson in the Eastern District, who used to march with us against the Vietnam War. When we brought the case to him, he made it quite clear that he would have liked to rule for us, but he considered himself bound by precedent in the Second Circuit.

Then, eventually, we won it on appeal, in the Second Circuit. It has now been held up in five or six other circuits and at the Supreme Court.

RATNER: Let's talk about that circuit for a second, because it was extraordinary. What you were saying there is that a person who was tortured in Paraguay, a Paraguayan national, tortured by a Paraguayan police official, that the family of the man who was tortured and killed could bring a suit in the United States. That's pretty extraordinary. Because I know you're a big person in international law, what was so important to you about that?

WEISS: It was not only the courts, but also the State Department. Remember, this was under Jimmy Carter. When I got up to argue that case before the Second Circuit, Judge Kaufman, of Rosenberg fame, interrupted me after the first two or three sentences and said, "Mr. Weiss, what does the State Department think of this case?"

I asked myself, "What's going on here?" I mean, I was taught in law school that we're supposed to have an independent judiciary here. But what I said to the judge was, "Well, there are people in the State Department who like this case, and there are people in the State Department who don't like it. But I don't think it should matter what people in the State Department think, because you're the judge."

Now as it happened, about five minutes after the hearing was over, Judge Kaufman told his clerk to write to the State Department and ask for the State Department's position. One of the people to whom this request came was a wonderful man named Charles Runyon, who used to be the assistant dean at Yale when I was there and who was a great proponent of human rights. That was the brief period when human rights were really being taken seriously by the State Department.

The brief that the State Department submitted supported the case, and I'm convinced that had it been the other way, we would have lost it. We didn't really win it before Judge Kaufman. We won it in the State Department.

RATNER: I think that's a really important point. Of course, the period was, again, Jimmy Carter's presidency, '77 to '81, right after the Vietnam War. It was a president who at least espoused human rights, and it was a special period, I think, in our American history. Now, Judge Kaufman did have some ringing language in that opinion, which you might want to tell our listeners.

WEISS: The ringing language was: "With this decision, the torturer, like the pirate of old, has become *hostus humani hentorus*, the enemy of all mankind." We lifted it from somewhere, and he lifted it out of our brief.

The case was the beginning of something which may well turn out to be the most important development in international law this century: universal jurisdiction.

This is the principle that some crimes are so heinous that they should be subject to trial in any country in the world.

We haven't quite gotten there yet, but we do have the alien tort statute in the United States. We have the International Criminal Court. We have an increasing number of countries which have enacted legislation to implement the principle of universal jurisdiction.

For instance, the German Universal Jurisdiction Law says that a crime, a war crime, a crime against humanity, aggression, or genocide, can be prosecuted by the German prosecutor, regardless of where it happens, and regardless of where the perpetrator is located.

Unfortunately, almost sixty cases have been brought on that so far in Germany, and not a single one has been followed up by the prosecutor. So that's a wonderful example of the hypocrisy of legislators and prosecutors.

RATNER: Of course, Peter and I and the Center for International Human Rights [European Center for Constitutional and Human Rights] are co-counsel in the Rumsfeld case in Germany, which was recently dismissed. Universal jurisdiction was the basis on which we brought it.

WEISS: Yes. I think we should mention—because we need a laugh here—the ground on which the case was dismissed both times.

The official ground of the prosecutor was that there was no reason to believe that Rumsfeld wouldn't be prosecuted in the United States.

SMITH: We wanted to talk to you about your work trying to stop nuclear proliferation. You're the president of an organization that's trying to bring about that through law, and you've been active in that for many decades.

WEISS: The first thing to do about it is to get away from the word, "non-proliferation," because non-proliferation, in the Nuclear Non-Proliferation Treaty of 1968, is another word for nuclear apartheid. In other words, the five official nuclear weapons states, which interestingly also happen to be the five states that have the veto in the Security Council—the U.S., France, the U.K., Russia, and China—want to hold onto their nuclear weapons, and they don't want anybody else to have them. Right? We got them. You can't get them. That's their view of the Non-Proliferation Treaty. That is a total violation of the treaty itself, of which one of my colleagues in this area always says, "Whenever you talk about it, you have to call it the 'Treaty for Non-Proliferation and for Total Nuclear Disarmament,'" because that's what it was intended to be. Article 6 of the treaty says, here's the deal: you guys, the rest of the world, stay away from nuclear weapons, and we, who have them, will negotiate in good faith to get rid of them.

That second part has been buried. Back in 1995, I was president of the International Association for Lawyers Against Nuclear Arms, which has chapters in quite a few countries. My colleagues in this country and in many other countries lobbied the General Assembly of the United Nations to put a question to the International Court of Justice, which is the highest tribunal for questions of international law in the world.

The question basically was, "Is the threat or use of nuclear weapons legal or illegal under international law?" That was based on the fact that international law prohibits many of the characteristics of nuclear weapons. The principle one being that there is no way to limit that weapon to what weapons are supposed to do: namely kill soldiers. There's no way to discriminate between soldiers and civilians if a nuclear weapon is ever used.

There are other things, like violations of neutrality and so forth. We got the majority of the General Assembly to put the question to the International Court. We had three weeks of hearings before the International Court of Justice in The Hague, where we were in touch with various governments that submitted briefs or argued in person before the court. More countries participated than in any previous case in the history of the International Court of Justice and its predecessor, the Permanent Court of International Arbitration, since 1922.

One interesting aspect of it was that countries testify or argue before the court in alphabetical order. And so the last two countries when we were there to argue were the United States and the U.K. Knowing that the judges are frequently influenced by the last presentations made to them, we had to do something. So what do we do? We got Zimbabwe. We stayed up all night with the local representative, and in the end Zimbabwe made a beautiful presentation to the court.

It was about nine months later that the judges came out with the ruling, saying in effect that the threat and use of nuclear weapons is generally illegal under international law. Then they did something remarkable.

The last sentence in this very long decision answered a question we hadn't even put to them. They affirmed that there is a general obligation, meaning an obligation binding on all countries in the world, to negotiate in good faith and pursue to a conclusion a treaty providing for the elimination of all nuclear weapons. The words, "in good faith," are in there, taken from Article 6 of the non-proliferation treaty.

At this point, we in the anti-nuclear legal community, or the anti-nuclear activist community, are considering going back to the court, and with the help again of the General Assembly, asking a new question. When the highest tribunal in the world dealing with international law questions has said that there is a general obligation to do something in good faith, how long can countries wait to implement this? Because it's been eleven years now.

MICHAEL RATNER: Peter, you've had a long and successful career, and won some really important cases. How do you look at the future? I would say, from our position at the Center, and from yours, there are some bleak things that have happened, certainly in this last period.

How do you keep going?

WEISS: If you've been associated with the Center for Constitutional Rights as long as I have been, which is since 1969, you have to have faith in the future. Because otherwise, we'd be wasting our time.

Things are pretty bleak. But as long as there are places like the Center, and people like the lawyers who work at the Center, and in other organizations that do Guantanamo work and human rights work, and so forth, I take a long view. I think at some point, human rights will become the architecture of society. I'm going to quote Justice Thurgood Marshall of the Supreme Court, who said that "the law is the glue that holds society together." So, you need the full implementation of human rights, all human rights for all people, as it says in the United Nations. But you also need lawyers who bring the kind of cases that we've been bringing at the Center. And you need judges who have the courage to deal with them.

Peter Weiss was interviewed on Law and Disorder *on August 6, 2007, by Michael Ratner and Michael Steven Smith. This interview has been edited and condensed.*

MEL WULF

Mel Wulf was the assistant legal director (1958–1962) and then the legal director (1962–1977) of the American Civil Liberties Union. He worked in Mississippi and on civil rights cases in 1961–62 and summer 1964 with the Lawyers Constitutional Defense Committee. He argued ten cases before the United States Supreme Court. He is now retired after having practiced law for fifty-four years.

MICHAEL RATNER: I want to start with the Philip Agee case. Agee was a former CIA agent who wrote a book called *Inside the Company,* which revealed a couple of hundred names of CIA people all over South and Central America. I want to bring it up first because I recently got a request saying, "Michael, the U.S. took away the passport from Ed Snowden. So we're sitting in Moscow without a U.S. passport." And they said, "Can't we bring a lawsuit to get Ed Snowden's passport back?" And I just typed them four letters: A-G-E-E. Why don't you tell us about why Snowden would have a very tough time getting his passport back?

MEL WULF: Well, he would. Phil Agee, as you said, was a dissident CIA agent who spent decades working against the CIA. He lost his passport because when dissidents took over the American embassy in Tehran in '79, the *New York Post* carried a story accusing Phil of helping the students who'd invaded the embassy to put together all the written material that had been shredded.

RATNER: How could he have done that?

WULF: Well, he didn't do it. That was another *New York Post* bald-faced lie. In any case, the State Department, based upon that story, revoked Agee's passport on national security grounds.

We started a lawsuit in the District of Columbia to get his passport back. We won it there based on a U.S. Supreme Court decision some years earlier on behalf of Rockwell Kent [a famous American artist who was represented by Leonard Boudin]. The government had revoked Kent's passport for political reasons but the Supreme Court declared that revocation unconstitutional on First Amendment grounds. So we thought we were in the catbird seat and started an action for Phil. We won it in the District Court; the government appealed and we won it again in the Court of Appeals, in the District of Columbia. When the government appealed again, the case went to the U.S. Supreme Court. Unfortunately, there, since they couldn't get Agee, they got his lawyer instead. They gave me a really, really hard time in that argument. They also reversed the Kent decision, saying Kent doesn't apply in this case. They didn't say exactly why, because it did apply, obviously. The vote went six to three to uphold the State Department's cancellation of Agee's passport. Agee was widely disliked in the Washington community as a well-known CIA dissident who would disclose the names of CIA agents.

I dare say if Snowden went the same route today, he would do even worse in this Supreme Court than I did. So I guess that's why Snowden won't get his passport back.

MICHAEL STEVEN SMITH: Mel, it strikes me that unlike Michael and me, you're a '50s radical. We would call ourselves '60s radicals, but you've got half a generation on us. How does a guy get your sensibilities coming up in the '50s out of Troy, New York?

WULF: My family were owners of a business in Troy. They made men's clothing and I often worked in the factory. I got to know the guys who worked on the floor, in the cutting room, and the women who worked on the sewing machines. And somehow or other, I don't know why, I sort of preferred the guys who were working on the floor rather than my father and his brothers who were working in the front office. I was for the worker and not for the bosses. And I've always been for the workers and not for the bosses, which I think is the distinguishing political factor in our world today: which side are you on? That was the basic background for the development, I think, of my left, liberal, or radical attitudes toward American political life.

RATNER: Let's move to the 1960s. How did you find yourself in the South?

WULF: Well, it was the beginning of the height of the civil rights movement and at that time, in 1958, I went to work at the American Civil Liberties Union [ACLU] as assistant legal director. In 1962 I was given the job of legal director of the ACLU. I started going down to Mississippi in '61 and '62, working with one of the two black lawyers who were then practicing in Mississippi, a wonderful guy named R. Jess Brown, who worked out of Jackson. He had called the ACLU out of the blue once, and I happened to answer that phone call. Jess had a capital case and he wanted some help. I went down to Jackson and tried that case with him. To call it a "trial" would be a vast overstatement but, in any case, we went ahead. Jess and I tried a couple of capital cases together around Mississippi, in Jackson, in Philadelphia, and in Vicksburg, I remember.

I continually argued the question of systematic exclusion of blacks from the jury. I finally got a case up to the Mississippi Supreme Court on that issue. In that court I said, "If you don't do it, the federal courts will." And they said, "Sit down, Mr. Wulf"—no, they actually said, "Sit down, Wulf—we've heard enough from you." But the fact of the matter is that for twelve or fifteen years, because of the work that Jess and I did on the exclusion issue there was not an execution in Mississippi of any African American, because the State conceded that exclusion tainted every conviction. But they weren't going to change. So, instead of giving these black guys the death penalty they sentenced them to life without parole. Still, it was a step in the right direction.

RATNER: That reminds me of a famous incident that happened in Columbia. We had James Meredith in the class, who was the first black man to desegregate a white university in Mississippi. A case came up where a black guy who, accused of raping a white woman in Mississippi or something, had only gotten life imprisonment. The professor says to the class, "Why do you think that black man only got life in prison?" And Meredith raises his hand and says, "Because he was innocent."

WULF: The summer of '64 saw the Voter Registration Project. We had heard that the National Lawyers Guild [NLG] was trying to find lawyers from around the country to go down and help out during the Mississippi summer. We at the ACLU thought that was a terrific idea and that we would do it also. We weren't going to do it in conjunction with the Guild because the ACLU and the Guild didn't get on very well.

RATNER: I was going to ask you about that. The Guild was looked at by many people, including some of your colleagues at the ACLU, as a Communist front. And they were worried that the Guild was getting a foothold, because the Communist Party had been active in desegregation for many years in the South. I remember, because I was a part of the Guild.

WULF: Well, the ACLU had a terrible history of anti-Communism. They expelled Elizabeth Gurley Flynn from the board because she was Communist Party [CP] member. For a long time, the ACLU had a despicable position on CP-ers within the ACLU. And the Guild looked at the ACLU as a bunch of bourgeois liberals, which we were.

SMITH: I want to say something in defense of the Guild. The original idea for the Guild to go down south in '64 came from Ernie Goodman, who was not a member of the Communist Party, and on various issues he stood up against the Communist Party inside of the Guild. And it was Ernie who organized that. In fact, the national office of the Lawyer's Guild moved from New York, which was more oriented toward the CP, to Detroit, where Ernie had a major law firm.

WULF: Picking up on the fact that the Guild was starting this summer project, we started the Lawyers Constitutional Defense Committee [LCDC] to duplicate what they were doing. And I think we ended up enlisting a lot more lawyers than the Guild did. We had two hundred lawyers who went down to

Mississippi that summer, for periods of a week or two, sometimes longer, to represent activists who were arrested while engaged in voter registration.

None of these lawyers were members of the Mississippi bar, obviously. When they appeared in court on behalf of their clients, the judge in the northern district was quite receptive to them, but the guy in the southern district was a real fascist. Most of the judges allowed these out-of-state lawyers to come and make some sort of presentation. But it wasn't so much their role as lawyers that was important to them, it was seeing first-hand what Mississippi was like back in 1964, when it was like the Third Reich.

RATNER: It still has some problems.

WULF: It was said some years ago that Mississippi in fact had more elected black officials than any other state in the union. So you've got to give them credit for something.

RATNER: Mel, proceeding along, I know you've argued ten cases before the United States Supreme Court. Let's talk about the Students for a Democratic Society [SDS] case.

WULF: I argued the only case on behalf of SDS that the U.S. Supreme Court ever heard. The SDS was a left-wing student group back in those days. The case was called *Healy v. James* [1972]. James was the president of a branch of the Connecticut state university system and Healy was a student there. The university had refused to allow a local group to organize on campus as an SDS membership organization. I won the case, and it was a good First Amendment decision. I think it was unanimous.

RATNER: I think you and our listeners will get a kick out of the opening paragraph of the brief, which basically says, "We mention briefly at the outset the setting in '69 and 1970. A climate of unrest prevailed on many college campuses. Widespread civil disobedience accompanied by seizure of buildings, vandalism, and arson. Some colleges had been shut down altogether, while at others files were looted and manuscripts destroyed. SDS chapters on some of those campuses had been a catalytic force during this period."

WULF: Exactly.

RATNER: We were representing a catalytic force, Mel. That gives you a sense of the times and where you were going in front of the court, which would have been in some way hostile to SDS, I would assume.

WULF: I had a pretty good reception on that case, as a matter of fact. Vastly different than the reception I had arguing Phil Agee's passport case.

SMITH: Mel, you took some bruises by some of these judges, and I want to ask you: of the various judges on the Supreme Court you've had to deal with, who did you admire the most?

WULF: Our favorite Catholic, William Brennan; Thurgood Marshall; Hugo Black who, as a young man, had been in the KKK; William O. Douglas; and Earl Warren, of course. That was the core of the liberal Supreme Court in its day, from the late '50s to the middle '60s or thereabouts, until Warren Burger took over.

RATNER: We grew up with that core. We had great expectations going forward as law students and lawyers that we would have a great court.

SMITH: And then it took a dive.

RATNER: Were most of your cases argued during that period?

WULF: I argued the first one in '63 and the last one in '82, so they spanned those years. But even with that very good court, they were not always helpful. Under the McCarran Act—the Subversive Activities Control Act [1950]—cases against Communists fared very badly compared to cases involving blacks. Our mantra was, "If you're red you lose. If you're black you win." That was true even of the Warren Court.

RATNER: The judge I worked for, Constance Baker Motley, argued ten cases like you in front of the Supreme Court. She won nine of them. So it just tells you how, at least on that point, the court was willing to give its imprimatur to black civil rights.

WULF: They were very good on that issue. And they did eventually throw out the membership provision of the Smith Act.

SMITH: Why has the Supreme Court, and lower federal courts as well, gotten to be so bad?

WULF: Perfectly clear. The presidents who appointed these right-wing guys wanted a different court, wanted to go to the other end of the spectrum of the Warren court. And I would like to take this opportunity, since I'm on the air and speaking publicly, to say that I think that Antonin Scalia is the worst judge in the history of the Supreme Court of the United States, followed by Clarence Thomas. Scalia is a pointy-headed right-winger—he's the worst guy. I don't know why Ruth Ginsburg is so friendly with him. They both like the opera. If I were her, I'd stay away.

Mel Wulf was interviewed on Law and Disorder *on November 4, 2013, by Michael Ratner and Michael Steven Smith. This interview has been edited and condensed.*

BRUCE WRIGHT (1917–2005)

With the appearance in the fall of 1996 of the long-awaited second volume of his autobiography, *Black Justice in a White World*, retired New York City judge Bruce Wright comes into focus as a significant figure in the heritage and history of our country, not only as a jurist and attorney, but as a humanist intellectual, a poet, and a humorist. Wright wanted to call the book *Memoirs of an Amnesiac*, but was overruled by his publisher, Lyle Stuart, who published Wright's first volume, *Black Robes, White Justice*, when no one else would. Exquisitely written, this memoir is to be relished all the more so for the poetry Wright puts into his prose, suffused as it is with a delighting wit.

"My life has been a series of events," he writes, "some remarkable." Indeed. Wright became a New York City judge relatively late in his life, unexpectedly appointed by Mayor John Lindsay in 1970. When Lindsay told him of his appointment, Wright, unbelieving, replied that he couldn't accept the judgeship because he did not have the money to pay for it.

He was then fifty-two years old. He had been a published poet, a lawyer, a decorated WWII combat veteran, an army deserter, a manager and adviser to jazz musicians, and an expatriate intellectual in Paris. He had collaborated with Langston Hughes in editing a book of Lincoln University poets and considered Hughes a confidant. Hughes introduced him to Zora Neale Hurston and Richard Wright, "an almost mythical figure in my mind."

Like many black Americans, Bruce Wright found the City of Light less oppressive, deserting the army on his way back to America from European combat, making the decision en route when a white officer looked at his medals and then, looking straight at him said, "I didn't know they allowed niggers to fight."

In Paris he met Gertrude Stein and James Baldwin, with whom he got drunk on scotch and ended up in a French hospital with a bleeding ulcer. It was also in Paris where he met the poet and future president of Senegal, Leopold Senghor, who regarded Wright as "his best American friend" and presented him as a "well-known black American poet." Senghor gave him a job on a publication of French colonial Africans, fed him, and introduced him "to dinners with courses and the necessity of wine with lunch and dinner." Through Senghor, with whom he maintained a lifelong friendship, often visiting him in Dakar, Wright came into contact with John Oliver Killens, Chester Himes, and Ralph Ellison.

Returning stateside and moving to Harlem, where he has lived for five decades, Wright knew Harlem Renaissance artists Romare Bearden, Charles Alson, and Aaron Douglas, whose murals of the African American experience decorate the Harlem library.

Wright was closely associated with the post–WWII jazz scene. The emergence of black nationalism in the northern urban ghettos in the 1950s coincided and interrelated with a revolution in black music called Bebop. The Beboppers were rebels, culturally and personally, if not overtly politically. They took jazz and stood it on its head, taking traditional "American classical music," the great gift of black America to the world, and elevating it to new levels of complexity and beauty. Bruce Wright, a rebel himself, identified and associated with the new music at its birth and was a manager and business adviser to great artists including Max Roach, Art Blakey, John Coltrane, Charles Mingus, Miles Davis, Horace Silver, Mary Lou Williams, and Sonny Rollins.

Wright's mother was Irish, one of thirteen children, whose ancestors came from Ireland around 1825, settling in Newark, New Jersey. Bruce was raised in Princeton, New Jersey, in a loving home with a brother and sister. His father was a black man from Monserrat, a Caribbean Island from which he emigrated because "there was nothing to do except haul water to Antigua." Wright remembers his mother as "a tall, handsome woman, jolly, and a moderate drinker. She seemed utterly at ease with the black neighbors among whom we always lived. My father, he was five feet four inches tall, a perfectly reasonable height for a pacifist. A survivor of World War I, he preached to me from childhood the virtues of imagined peace."

Wright recalls an incident in Washington, D.C., where he was touring with his mother. A toilet had a sign over it advising "Whites Only." Bruce asked his mom to take a photo. Just then a cop approached. "Is he bothering you?" the officer inquired of his mother. "He's been bothering me for twenty-eight years."

When his parents died they were buried in the Princeton Cemetery. "There, the dead were separated, even as they had been in life, on the basis of race. There was a 'Negro' section and a white section. My mother and her older sister, my Aunt Catherine, are buried in the white section. My father lies in the same obscurity he knew in life, in the areas reserved for the black dead."

Wright's parents respected education. He was a fine student as well as an excellent athlete, winning the statewide high school mile run. His track coach, Irwin Weiss, arranged for a scholarship to Princeton. He would be the first person in either branch of the family to attend college. Bruce stood in the registration line with his fellow freshmen on opening day. He was pulled from the group and taken to the office of Radcliffe Heermance, the dean of admissions. "He looked down upon me as though I was a disgusting laboratory specimen. He was the first man ever to address me as 'mister.' 'Mr. Wright,' he scolded, 'Mr. Weiss never told us you were colored when your scholarship was awarded.'" He ordered Wright to find a college "of your own kind" and directed an upperclassman to take him to Robert Russell Wicks, the dean of the chapel. Wicks "wanted to know if I was like a certain Communist in the town of Princeton who was always seeking entrance to places where he was not wanted . . . He then indicated that the conference was concluded. Since that confrontation I have never since trusted white men with three names." His faith in hard study and love of learning, in fairness and in patriotism were shattered in what "was one of the most destructive moments of my life."

His father, without a trace of anger, said simply, "We'll just have to find another college for him." His mother suggested that after Presbyterian Princeton they try Catholic Notre Dame. Wright was rejected from there on the grounds laid out by Bishop John F. O'Hara, then presiding over the Army and Navy Diocese in the segregated armed forces. The Bishop wrote that, "We northern Catholics naturally deplore any such thing as race discrimination, but at the same time, we have to recognize the feelings of these Southern boys [at Notre Dame] with whom race prejudice is strong." "That response," said Bruce Wright, "coupled with the Princeton rejection, was the beginning of my skepticism and ultimate rejection of Christianity." Wright finally graduated from Lincoln University in Pennsylvania, which in 1866 was one of the first integrated colleges in America.

At the onset of World War II he supported young black civil rights attorney Conrad Lynn's historic lawsuit on behalf of Lynn's brother, Sam, which sought to enjoin the government from drafting blacks into a segregated army. "Quite apart from any technical grounds, it seemed ridiculous to draft American troops to fight against Hitler's brand of racism while America practiced its own." Then Wright himself was drafted and "sent off—first to Fort Dix and later to a dreadful hinterland in rural Alabama called Fort Rucker." Black draftees called it Mother Rucker.

He was then twenty-three years old. He hoped fighting abroad would have a good effect for black people at home. At first Wright was put into a labor battalion. Blacks were not allowed in combat positions. Conrad Lynn was also drafted and spent weeks shoveling out the latrine. This changed at the war's end. Wright volunteered to fight, was shot and wounded, hospitalized, and returned to the front line. He saved a white soldier, who, as it turned out, was later to die of his wounds.

During the war, a book of his poetry, *From the Shaken Tower,* was published in England and it was at that time also that he began his collaboration with Langston Hughes.

After eighteen months in Paris, he was arrested for desertion, but wiggled out of the charge, ridiculing the "eighteen months" that was written on the charge, saying it was a typo, and announcing that truly it was "eighteen weeks." He then entered and completed New York Law School.

Wright writes about his legal and judicial exploits in *Black Robe, White Justice*. Prentice Hall originally contracted for that book, paying Wright $13,000, but after their lawyers reviewed it, they refused to go forward with its printing. They never asked for the $13,000 back.

Wright ran afoul of the police and the prosecutors when he refused to rubber stamp routinely high bail requests, that not only denied the accused the right to prepare his own defense but worked in practice as preventative detention. When he released an accused cop killer (later acquitted), the Policeman's Benevolent Association went ballistic. The tabloid press dubbed him "Turn 'em Loose Bruce."

A demonstration was called in his defense. Hundreds gathered to support him in front of the downtown municipal building. When his judgeship was not renewed, he ran for the Civil Court from Harlem and won a ten-year term. He was also extremely popular among lawyers who appeared before him because of his intelligence and courtesy. Bruce Wright is a well-known figure in Harlem. The encomium that he liked best was given him the day a car knocked him off his bicycle, seriously injuring him. As Wright lay in the street, a passerby looked down at him and said, "Oh shit, it's the judge."

Wright prefaces *Black Justice in a White World* with a quote from New School professor Horace Keeler who reminds each new class that "The world we live in is not meant for us, nor us for it." He recalls standing on the beach at Coney Island looking eastward toward Ireland and Africa from where his ancestors hailed, knowing he couldn't go back (where in Ireland? Africa? What country? What village?), reflecting on the irony of his situation, coming to life in a black skin, making his way in racist America, knowing, with Thomas Wolfe, that "you can't go home again." But you can write, summing it all up, which Bruce Wright has done with dignity and aplomb, gifting us with a memoir to be treasured.

Originally published in Michael Steven Smith, Lawyers You'll Like: Putting Human Rights First *(Union City, N.J.: Smyrna Press, 1999).*

MYRON BELDOCK

Myron Beldock (1929–2016) was a Brooklyn-born New York City civil rights lawyer and partner in the prestigious progressive law firm Beldock, Levine, and Hoffman. He was famous for defending "lost causes," none more so than the case of Rubin "Hurricane" Carter.

When Carter died at age seventy-six, he had become an international symbol of racial injustice after his murder conviction put him in prison in New Jersey for nineteen years. Carter was arrested for a triple murder in his hometown of Paterson, New Jersey. At that time he was the number-one contender for the middleweight boxing championship of the world and a public supporter of Malcolm X.

He was convicted in 1967 by an all-white jury and sentenced to three consecutive life sentences. In 1976, the New Jersey State Supreme Court overturned his conviction on the grounds that the state withheld material evidence from the defense. But Carter was convicted again in a second trial that year.

Carter garnered wide public support. Bob Dylan wrote a song about him that was premiered at a huge support rally in Madison Square Garden.

In 1985, the second conviction was overturned by a U.S. District Court judge who concluded that the state had made an unconstitutional appeal to racial prejudice. In 1988, the Passaic, New Jersey prosecutor's office dropped all charges against Carter.

I interviewed Carter several times, and helped form a defense committee for him at the time of his second trial. Myron Beldock represented Carter in his final appeal, and was interviewed by us shortly before Beldock's death.

HEIDI BOGHOSIAN: How did you get involved in the Carter case?

MYRON BELDOCK: After Rubin and [co-defendant] John Artis were defeated in the first trial, Rubin started his campaign to get out of jail and wrote his book, *The Sixteenth Round.* Ultimately in 1974, when the supposed eyewitnesses recanted their testimonies, someone asked me whether I was interested in representing Rubin. I had just finished seven years working on another case and really didn't want to get involved in another long battle. But I went to see Rubin. He was charismatic and powerful, a great thinker. He was a very, very intellectually strong person, as well as being spiritually strong. I was drawn into his ambience and then we went off.

The killings were shotgun and pistol shootings of these three people. The original witnesses were two—I would say—criminal types, who were involved in breaking into a factory a block away at the time of the shootings in 1966. The first conviction was set aside because it turned out that the prosecution had been trading benefits to those particular people for their stories. Their original information, and all the original information, described people completely different than Rubin and John.

One of the people who ultimately died, in fact two of them, saw Rubin and John in the hospital that night. They did not identify them. It was a typical high-profile case, where you get people who are vulnerable and easily manipulated to falsely testify because of their need for their own benefits.

It went to trial again in 1975. By this time, the atmosphere had changed. There was a new prosecutor. They came up with the theory that this was actually a racial revenge killing. Earlier on the night of the killing, a white former bar owner had shot and killed the black man who had purchased the bar from him. That was always known. No motive had been attributed to the killings in the first trial. But in the second trial, really based upon nothing but speculation and bias, they argued persuasively to the jury that this was really a racial revenge killing; that the black people went into the white bar, the Lafayette Bar, to avenge the killing of the black person by the white former bar owner. That was one of the ultimate reasons why many, many years later the convictions were set aside.

The other reason was the one I was most prominently involved in. At the second trial, Mr. Bello, who was the only supposed eyewitness who testified—there were two of them at the first trial—was being questioned by me on the stand as to why he had recanted his recantation. The prosecution had persuaded him to revert to the story he told at the first trial, identifying Rubin and John.

I was trying to establish that they had falsely manipulated him when I was pulled into the chambers along with my co-counselor, Lewis Steel, who represented John Artis, and told that if I questioned him further, the jury would learn that he had passed a lie detector test supporting what he had said at the first trial, supporting his identification. We did have that test and it seemed like that was the result, because that's the way it was written.

In fact, that was a fraud. Just like the first trial, it was a total cheat. The polygraph results were completely the opposite of what they were purported to be. Just before the sentencing in the second trial, 1976, I called the polygrapher, who we thought was an enemy, as he was in a sense, but I had info on him from a well-known New York City investigator. I said, "Hey, John said I could call you and speak to you, and give you my name, and that you can rely on me." Then all of a sudden, he tells me the results of the test were the opposite of what they were purported to be.

I thought we could win. We didn't win then. That was 1976. It was 1985 when we finally got a federal judge to recognize these two basic flaws in the prosecution. That was Judge [Haddon Lee] Sarokin who went over all the years of all the evidence and came to the conclusion that we were essentially cheated. I use the word "cheated" because that's what it was. You know, the prosecutors in that case, two of them became judges, rewarded for what they did.

MICHAEL STEVEN SMITH: Let me ask you: The two key elements in being cheated were, one, the false lie detector results, and what was the other one?

BELDOCK: That John and Rubin killed the white people at the Lafayette Bar to retaliate from the earlier shooting of a black bartender that night by the white former bar owner. There's no evidence that John or Rubin were involved in being biased against white people. Just the opposite. They both had lots of relationships with white people. There was just no evidentiary basis for this argument.

Remember, this is a community that was shocked by the killings. There were three of their own who were killed, one who survived. Rubin was not a popular person. He had been an outspoken civil rights person. There were false rumors about his being a person who would support killing people, killing white people. It was a cesspool of rumors without any evidentiary basis that led to the prosecution.

I can tell you, as one who was there, that the entire community, almost, in the State of New Jersey, treated us like we were the devil. We were enemies. It was the coldest community reception I ever encountered anyplace.

SMITH: One of the things that was so striking in this case was the degree of corruption in the State of New Jersey, I suppose you could say it hasn't changed much with Chris Christie. The prosecutor in Essex County was an attorney named Byrne, who later became governor. Rubin said that it was Byrne who arranged to give the lighter sentence to Bello and Bradley in exchange for their testimony. Rubin said, "This thing is corrupt from top to bottom."

BELDOCK: I think it was corrupt, but I don't know about the Byrne angle. They certainly gave benefits to both Bello and Bradley, who had been the original witnesses, by not prosecuting them, or not putting them in jail for their various crimes. They were very unreliable witnesses. Bello was an exceedingly dishonest person. The whole story about the lie detector test is absurd because he was an immoral kind of person who didn't care about the truth. That was established over the years in many investigations, in many aspects of the case.

SMITH: Let's talk about Rubin and the work that he did. It seems to me, without being melodramatic, that he was truly a tragic and heroic figure. After you, with your great legal skills, got him out of prison, he then moved up to Canada and did work supporting innocent people.

BELDOCK: He got dedicated in two different organizations: the Association in Defense of the Wrongfully Convicted in Canada and then a group called the Innocence Project. He continued to do that in his own right until the end of his life. He was interested in supporting a convicted person in Kings County and had been fighting to help get him out. He did what he thought he should do to return to the world his principled good efforts to set aside injustices.

Rubin was an extraordinary person. He participated with us in the defense of his case and would vet the briefs that we sent. We used to have a relay between Rahway Prison and my office sending him drafts. We would get the comments back. He was a very unusual client.

He was a hero to a lot of the prisoners. Rubin refused to act like a prisoner because he wasn't anyone who was guilty, he said. He didn't eat prison food. He didn't take prison assignments. He didn't wear prison clothes. Somehow or other, he was able to pull that off. Some of the guards even supported him because they recognized his principled stand.

Early on, when one of our appeals failed (I can't remember whether it was one of the earlier appeals), Rubin essentially had an emotional breakdown in prison, a mental breakdown, and he was hallucinating, beyond the depths of despair. There was a white prisoner—well known because of his crime—who took Rubin aside, nurtured Rubin through that time. He came back even stronger. You can't imagine what a strong person he was.

After the second conviction, when our lives were so bleak, we met in a prison basement in New Jersey, and we were weak in spirit. But after that second conviction, Rubin did an analysis of all the evidence at the second trial on big, big boards, with little flip cards so that you'd look under what the prosecution claimed and what the impeachment evidence was. I still have it. It's a unique document. It's 4' x 5' wide and has many, many boxes. That's when I knew he was really coming back. As I said, he was a participant in his case like no other client I've ever had.

SMITH: He truly was extraordinary. He didn't get much of an education. He was in juvenile prisons as a young person. His father was a deacon or a minister in the church, I think. He had a real moral sense to him. When Malcolm X came around, Rubin recognized Malcolm's moral authority, identified with him. I think that may have been one of the things that got him into trouble, because *Life* magazine wrote an article linking the two.

BELDOCK: Yes. He was portrayed as a dangerous rebel. That certainly didn't make him popular in the community in Paterson, New Jersey, at least for some elements of the community. He had a lot of white friends, too. People think of it as being another time. I have been practicing law long enough, so I don't think anything changes. The same kind of bias runs deep throughout the community. It's just masked somewhat differently, as we see from current events.

Myron Beldock was interviewed on Law and Disorder *on February 15, 2016, by Michael Steven Smith and Heidi Boghosian. This interview has been edited and condensed.*

CONRAD JOSEPH LYNN (1908–1995)

Cancer claimed Conrad Lynn, who passed away in his bungalow home in rural Rockland County, north of New York City. He was eighty-seven years old and had been an extraordinary movement lawyer, political thinker, and activist since he joined the Young Communist League as a student at Syracuse University in 1928.

He intended to enter the church, but became a minister with a different mission. "Understand this about my father," his son Alexander said as he memorialized him, "he was a Communist." His communism was like that of the early Christian church in that it stemmed "from humans having a sense of responsibility for one another."

Conrad had been a founder of both the National Lawyers Guild and the National Conference of Black Lawyers. Several hundred friends, fellow lawyers, judges, family members, and comrades joined him in a magnificent memorial meeting at City College in New York City.

Judge Bruce Wright said he was "a one-man civil rights movement long before it became popular, long before others joined in it. Although he was of small stature Conrad had the heart of a lion." He laughed heartily with eyes smiling behind thick glasses. And he laughed a lot. Though only 5'4", Conrad had muscled, large, athletic legs. Until nearly the end he sprinted for exercise rather than jogging and he insisted on cutting his own firewood, his motto being, "A man who chops his own wood is warmed twice by the fire."

He read widely and all the time. Conversation with Conrad was "an event," as his friends and family recalled. He laced his observations with quotes from Kipling and Longfellow to C.L.R. James and Franz Fanon and, of course, the Bible.

His fascinating autobiography is titled *There Is A Fountain*, a line from an old Protestant hymn. He devoured newspapers and was current with the global and local political situation. He talked politics in Harlem with Adam Powell, Paul Robeson, and especially his friend Malcolm X. Conrad shared with Malcolm X a revolutionary internationalist view of the world and met with him regularly. He saw Malcolm X developing politically, an evolution for which Conrad believed he was assassinated.

Speaking of his accomplishments, Haywood Burns recalled that "the litany goes back six decades." He recounted some of Conrad's battles.

In 1943, on behalf of his brother, Samuel, Conrad brought the first suit to desegregate the United States Army. At that time black people were consigned to menial jobs, like Conrad, who spent weeks shoveling out the latrine.

Samuel Lynn, Lieut. Colonel USAF Retired, told the meeting that "Conrad realized that the political and corporate leaders of America never accepted the release from slavery of African Americans."

Although Conrad lost the army suit, Haywood recounted that Conrad helped organize and participated in the first freedom ride to desegregate interstate travel and accommodations in 1947 (fourteen years before the better-known freedom rides of 1961 took on Jim Crow). Conrad was the first person arrested in Virginia when he held strong, refusing to move, sitting in the front seat of a bus in the teeth of a mob of angry whites and Southern cops. He was arrested and convicted, not for riding in the front, but for disorderly conduct, a conviction that was reversed on appeal after the bus driver testified that Conrad was not disorderly.

Burns spoke of Conrad defending the Puerto Rican *independentistas* Lolita Lebron and Alibizo Campos. Lebron, who had participated in an armed attack on Congress, sent a message to the meeting affirming that "Conrad was a great man for whom I felt a very great affection."

Conrad defended Black Panther victims of New York City's notorious Red Squad.

During the same period he was active in the movement against the war in Vietnam, representing draft resisters, frequently speaking at campuses and meetings, and even traveling illegally to North Vietnam as an investigator for the prestigious and influential Bertrand Russell War Crimes Tribunal.

One of the most well-known cases Conrad Lynn was associated with was the case of the Harlem Six, which he tried with his friend Bill Kunstler, who died a month before Conrad. The Six were black teenagers falsely convicted of murder in the 1960s and vindicated only after an eight-year legal battle.

Conrad was the chief lawyer in the infamous 1958 "Kissing Case," which became an international scandal. Two Monroe County, North Carolina, African American children, ages eight and ten, were convicted and imprisoned for being kissed on the cheek by a white child. Monroe County was and is controlled by the Jesse Helms family. The children were terrorized and scarred for life. Conrad took an appeal of their case, which was lost. It was only with the intervention of Eleanor Roosevelt, who cried when Conrad told her what happened, that the children were freed.

Conrad Lynn's last political act was to help organize persons from conservative Rockland County to go to the nation's capital to participate in the Million Man March. The group decided to call itself the Conrad Lynn Brigade for Social Justice in honor of Conrad, who was too sick to go himself. Conrad's friend Edmund Gordon described the brigade at the memorial meeting:

"When about 250 of us, friends and neighbors from Rockland County arrived in Washington, and joined that mass of humanity—both genders, diverse ethnic groups, various religious beliefs, different sexual orientations, different political beliefs and affiliations—gathered there in the spirit of reconciliation, atonement and responsibility, we knew that we had become a part of a renewed and powerful human struggle. We knew that Conrad's spirit and we were in the right place. We were convinced that our efforts at organizing and to advance and maintain social justice must continue."

Although Conrad was in various political parties over his lifetime his activity was mostly outside of a party framework. He quietly left the Young Communist League where he was a member as a student at Syracuse University in the late '20s. He could not abide by their "Black Belt" theory, which called for a separate black country in the American South. From family ties he said he knew the mind of the Southern black and thought the Moscow-inspired plan to be wholly impractical.

A few years later in New York City he joined the parent of the YCL, the Communist Party, only to quit it several years later in the late '30s. The Trinidad oil workers were on strike but the CP's solidarity was less than lukewarm so as not to upset its popular front alliance with Roosevelt. Conrad, always the internationalist, quit. Then the CP held a trial and expelled him.

Conrad was next briefly in the Socialist Workers Party (SWP) but left, writing that he thought it to be "doctrinaire." He supported the SWP and came to its defense in the 1941 Smith Act prosecution. Lynn wrote about how Paul Robeson, an enthusiastic supporter of the government's case, later came over to Conrad saying that he had made a mistake.

Conrad was a great admirer of C.L.R. James and was for a while in the milieu of the Workers Party. He drifted away, he reports, when a Workers Party leader expressed support of the Rapp-Cordet Committee's persecution of teachers in New York City who were members of the Communist Party. Many of them were driven out of education.

Conrad was consistently nonsectarian. He worked closely with the SWP in the late '50s, supporting the intransigent and courageous black leader in Monroe County, North Carolina, Robert Williams.

Like the SWP, he was quick to support independent black political action and was an enthusiastic leader of the New York branch of the Freedom Now Party.

Originally published in Michael Steven Smith, Lawyers You'll Like: Putting Human Rights First *(Union City, N.J.: Smyrna Press, 1999).*

RAMSEY CLARK

Ramsey Clark (b. 1927) was admitted to the Texas bar in 1950. He was the U.S. attorney general in Lyndon Johnson's cabinet and an important figure in the civil rights movement of the '60s. Clark broke with Johnson over his opposition to the war in Vietnam and has remained a dissident activist ever since, believing in the rule of law and the right of everyone to legal counsel, regardless of the nature of the charges against them.

CLARK: I grew up in a legal family in Texas. My father was a lawyer—in the beginning he was not in politics. He hitched his wagon to a fellow named Bill McCraw, who was about the best speaker I ever heard. His Sunday school class was so big, so popular, that kids were standing on tables. Spontaneous speaker. He ran for district attorney of Dallas County, and became the head of the civil division there. Then he ran for attorney general of Texas. Dad stayed in Dallas. McCraw ran for governor and got defeated, and by that time Dad decided he wanted to get into federal government. In 1937, when I was about eight years old, he got a job in the Department of Justice in the War Risk Litigation section, which was litigating veterans' claims from World War I.

I joined the Marines when I was seventeen and got out when I was eighteen. I saw a lot of misery and poverty, saw the destruction of World War II. Saw violence, coarse discipline.

I loved the guys I was with, but I didn't like the system, which is a system of absolute obedience to authority. When I got back, I started at the University of Texas under the GI Bill. I spent two and a half years there, got married to Georgia, my wife. Then Robert Hutchins at the University of Chicago caught my eye. I saw a picture of him in *Time* magazine in a football suit—and he had abolished football at the University of Chicago. And the year after, Jay Berwanger was the only All-American football player that ever came out of the University of Chicago, I think. What makes more nonsense than mixing football with higher education? Georgia and I went up to Chicago. In Chicago, they were still investigating Communists, which was a big thing in the '30s. Hutchins was an inspiring guy. I worked with him until he died. He created the Center for Study of Democratic Institutions out in Santa Barbara. People just went out there and thought about things, wrote about them, and tried to influence and persuade people.

While I was in law school there, Dad was appointed to the Supreme Court. I took a class there with Ed Levy on anti-trust law. In Texas, that was a big subject. Popular opinion was that you could still harness capitalism if you could break it up and keep it small—don't let 'em get a head start. And in fact, there were no national banks in Texas until after I left. We wouldn't let 'em in. Now they're all national or international.

I went back to Texas to practice law for about nine years. I became a main member in a firm and was doing criminal law and personal injury. I was doing pretty good, but then I came to realize that all I was doing was fighting over people's money for them, and I wanted something better to do. The Kennedy campaign caught my eye at the time. It seemed exciting. I was in a protracted automobile parts Federal Trade litigation at the time. I didn't do any campaigning because I didn't know anybody.

But I had come to know [Supreme Court Justice] William O. Douglas—he was a hero of mine. He was a close friend of Robert Hutchins. And [Congressman] Sam Rayburn, who was from Bonham, Texas; he was my best buddy when I was at the University of Texas. As soon as the election was over, they both talked to President Kennedy and Robert Kennedy for me. And in late November they said, "We'd like for you to join." So, I went up in January of '61 at the beginning of the administration, and was assigned by Byron White to the Lands Division, as it was called then. It was natural resources, public lands, and the environment. We filed the first water pollution cases in the history of the United States. Then the civil rights movement started, and I was one of the youngest and from the South. Bob White put me into civil rights. I went down to the South with civil rights activist James Meredith, who was to integrate the University of Mississippi. I went to Ole Miss (as the University of Mississippi was called) and could easily pass for a grad student. I would sit in the cafeteria and I couldn't believe what these pretty little young Mississippi gals were saying about Meredith. I hadn't heard language like that, and I was shocked. I remember once he said, "I want to go bowling." Well, there were no bowling alleys around there, so we had to go to Jackson. And boy, we had to take the 101st Airborne Division along, which is still on the campus at Ole Miss, to protect him. We sent 13,000 troops in. The campus had about 4,500 students, and the town had about 5,000. The theory was the power doctrine; you've got to have overwhelming force. By March of '63, they wanted to break it down to 2,000 soldiers. And I said, "That's ridiculous, you shouldn't have any soldiers on your campus anyway. This is supposed to be the United States of America." We finally got marshals. The Marshals Service at that time was old guys, they were all political appointees, friends of senators. They were good-hearted fellas, but they couldn't walk a hundred yards in a minute and a half. Still, they were providing part of the protection, and after that everything was fine. Meredith graduated.

In Mississippi, I was put in charge of integrating all of the schools, desegregating for the first time in the South of '63, which was an incredibly interesting experience in many ways. I started out with Baton Rouge. A judge named Gordon West was in charge, and he wouldn't meet with me. I found out he was on the golf links one day, and I went out there and he said, "I'm playing golf, go away." Literally, the guy wouldn't meet the person responsible for protecting his order when the kids got into school in September. I met with the African American leadership, and such as it was, they had to keep their heads down; this was 1963. I met with the sheriff's office, the local police department, the mayor, the head of the school district, the school principal. I met and tried to talk with everyone about how important it was that everybody be respectful and accept what's right and what the law requires.

I went from there to Savannah, Georgia and Charleston, South Carolina. The school board there was just awful, unbelievable. And here these are first graders. Beautiful little children, poor and frightened. Families frightened. And then President Kennedy was killed that fall. Fall of 1963. I thought I'd never be happy again. And for a long time, I couldn't go over the Memorial Bridge and see the eternal flame there without shedding a tear. But now, I don't know if it's age or time, or what it is, but I don't feel it like I did. I guess maybe because I've seen so much suffering and tragedy.

In September of '64, nearly a year after the president's murder, I flew up to New York with Bob Kennedy. We landed at Marine Terminal, drove into what was at the time a nice little guard armory on 33rd and Park Avenue, and as we were getting out of the car they said, "Hurry, hurry, they're waiting for ya." We get into the armory and they're taking us upstairs, and as soon as we get to the top of the stairs I hear a guy yelling, "Nominations are now in order for the United States Senate. (*Bang of a gavel.*) Do I hear a nomination?" A voice says, "I nominate Robert F. Kennedy." And I hear a second bang. "Nominations are now closed."

MICHAEL RATNER: This was the Democratic State Convention.

CLARK: In September of '64, yes. And that night, when I came into the hotel, Bob (Kennedy) was laying on his back on the floor, and he said, "How'd you like that convention? That's democracy in action." I said, "We gotta do something to change that."

I ran for Senate in New York, in 1974. The convention was in Niagara Falls. I was nominated by Frank Serpico. And he was fantastically popular at the time—this was just after the movie *Serpico* had come out. I remember Howard

J. Samuels was nominated for governor, and I walked into this big room where they were having a celebration, and everybody is crowded around Samuels, and Serpico was with me. And they all came running to see Serpico, and poor old Sam was left standing over there by himself, and I was left standing by myself; it was everybody around Serpico. It was so sad, because people got up and left. Beautiful guy, Sam. He was like a piece of carved mahogany, with this booming voice; and people just got up and started leaving. Then I got up and said, "I withdraw the nomination. I respect all of you, but this isn't the democratic process." We went out and got 150,000 signatures, won the ballot and won the Democratic Primary. Got more than half the votes. We lost the election, though. Jacob Javits became senator. But I had more votes on the Democratic line than Javits had on the Republican line. There were these two Independent parties, the Liberal and the Conservative, and neither one of them would let me into the convention. He got both of them, and they took him over. I went Upstate, and I said, "We've got to abolish handguns, absolutely abolish them, they only kill people—and licensed long guns and ammunition, and stop all the killing with guns." Went to Grumman [Aircraft] on Long Island, and said, 'War is a terrible thing, you're making a plane that kills people, and we ought to close the plant down."

RATNER: Would have been great had you been in the Senate.

CLARK: I had been nominated in February of '65 to be deputy attorney general. Nick Katzenbach, who had been deputy after Byron White went on the [Supreme] Court, in '62, became attorney general.

President Johnson called me one night and said, "I want you to know that I can't appoint you to attorney general: I'm from Texas, you're from Texas, there's too many Texans." I took him at his word. So that fall, there was a lot of action because we had a very thin staff, because there had been resignations, a vacancy at the solicitor general's office, criminal division. There were four divisions that had vacancies, including the attorney general. So, I was both deputy and acting attorney general. We had a major crime bill that brought a lot of heat on President Johnson. He vetoed the D.C. crime bill because it had wiretapping provisions that we opposed. Then I sent over about five or six hundred pardons and commutation applications that had been sitting around there for a long time. I read every one of them. I don't think I turned any down. And I'll be darned if he didn't sign them. He must have thought, "This knucklehead, he must know what he's doing." He caught hell for it. Then in February of '65, he called me over one day and said, "I'm going to nominate you to be attorney general." And he punched a button under his desk and said to tell the press to come in. And the press came charging in. I was in a state of shock. I was only thirty-seven.

I brought the Department of Justice against the death penalty. I opposed all wiretapping. I had been test-firing on those issues, so the real question was what was going to happen when my name went up. When I got out of the press conference, I went to the phone and called the [Supreme] Court. I told my father's secretary, "Tell Dad." Well, he knew about it already, in fact. He said, "Before you talk to him, your father has announced his retirement." So, we never had a chance to even talk about it. Now, there's been a lot of speculation as to why he [LBJ] appointed me: I think he apparently couldn't find the right person he wanted (he'd wanted Thurgood Marshall); he was getting pressure from people; and he thought he probably would just appoint me. I really don't know what it was.

Ramsey Clark was interviewed on Law and Disorder *on April 28, 2008, by Michael Ratner, Michael Steven Smith, and Heidi Boghosian. This interview has been edited and condensed.*

LYNNE STEWART

Lynne Stewart (1939–2017) was a teacher and librarian before becoming a lawyer. She lived and raised her family on the Lower East Side of Manhattan, where she practiced law in the community, representing everybody from tenants about to be evicted to accused criminal defendants.

She, along with Ramsey Clark and Abdeen Jabara, took on the defense of New Jersey blind cleric Sheikh Omar Abdel Rahman, who was falsely accused and convicted of conspiring to blow up New York City landmarks and sent to federal prison in Minnesota in 1995, where he died.

In an effort to keep his name in front of the public, Stewart visited her client in prison and issued a press release concerning a cease-fire in Egypt between the government there and the opposition Islamic Group that Rahman supported.

Her actions violated a prison regulation and she was told to stop.

Two years later, after the terrorist attacks on 9/11, President George W. Bush's attorney general, John Ashcroft, decided to make an example out of Stewart and had her indicted for conspiracy to materially aid terrorism. Ashcroft flew to New York City in 2002 and announced the indictment on a popular late-night television show hosted by David Letterman, thus prejudicing the chance of a fair trial. The government's twisted theory violated the First Amendment by positing that a press release supported terrorism.

The Bush administration selected and prosecuted Lynne Stewart to make an example out of her and to scare and intimidate lawyers who would stand up for clients accused of terrorism-related charges.

Stewart was tried, in a courthouse not far from where the Twin Towers once stood, by an anonymous sequestered jury brought to court each day in a police van surrounded by guards. An atmosphere of fear was all-pervasive. Huge photographs of Osama bin Laden were flashed on the wall of the courtroom. Not a single witness testified that Lynne Stewart had any connection to any terrorist activity anywhere.

Although she was ably defended by a team of stellar movement lawyers, including Michael Tigar, Ellen Yaroshefsky, Jill Shellow Levine, and Liz Fink, she was convicted of aiding terrorism because of the press release.

One juror, a black woman, complained afterward that she felt that the other jurors would get her if she did not vote for the conviction. The show trial had taken place in the same courtroom where Julius and Ethel Rosenberg were framed and sentenced to death on the false charge of giving the secret of the atomic bomb to Russia.

Lynne was sentenced in 2006 by Judge John Koeltl to twenty-eight months in prison. She was disbarred as a felon. She had recently been treated for breast cancer, which was to recur when she was incarcerated.

The government appealed the sentence, taking the position that it was far too short. The appellate court agreed and sent the case back to Judge Koeltl for resentencing, demanding he give the seventy-year-old grandmother thirty years.

When she was asked by Amy Goodman on the news show Democracy Now! *whether she would do it again, Lynne answered, "Yes." The appellate court wrote that she showed no remorse. President George W. Bush's cousin, Judge John Walker, sat on the appellate court and was particularly enraged against Stewart.*

After a hearing attended by hundreds of Stewart supporters, Judge Koeltl sentenced her to ten years, a virtual death sentence. The audience of supporters in the court let out a collective gasp. Her granddaughter shrieked. Attorney Levine rose to question the judge as to why he did it. He answered that he was ordered to.

Stewart received broad support, mostly from the left. Her husband, the black activist Ralph Poynter, was a steady presence by her side. Mainstream attorneys shunned the case.

Lynne Stewart was sent to a prison hospital in Texas. She served four years. The cancer came back, likely a result of stress. For nine long months, Ralph Poynter led a relentless international campaign to win compassionate release. An online petition received 85,000 signatures and the support of prominent voices like Archbishop Desmond Tutu, Noam Chomsky, and Dick Gregory. Finally, Lynne's application was approved by the Bureau of Prisons and quickly signed by Judge Koeltl on New Year's Eve 2013. The next day, the then seventy-four-year-old grandmother arrived at LaGuardia Airport.

In a letter to Judge Koeltl, Lynne wrote, "I do not intend to go 'gentle into that good night,' as Dylan Thomas wrote. There is much to be done in this world. I do know that I do not want to die in prison—a strange and loveless place . . . I want to where all is familiar . . . in a word, home."

She lived another three years and three months actively organizing and speaking. She was a woman of extraordinary ability, courage, virtue, grace, and kindness.

MICHAEL STEVEN SMITH: We're here to talk about the January 28th appellate oral argument in the Second Circuit Court of Appeals here in New York City.

HEIDI BOGHOSIAN: Let's just do a brief review. In 2002 [then U.S. attorney general John] Ashcroft announced an indictment against you, Lynne.

LYNNE STEWART: Right, for a press release that I had made to Reuters in 2000. During the Reno administration. Pat Fitzgerald, [the prosecutor] of Valerie Plame fame, was the head of anti-terrorism in the Southern District [of New York] at that point, and he's the one who called me and told me that I had violated a set of prison regulations, known as SAMs [Special Administrative Measures], by virtue of speaking to the media on behalf of my client. Within, I would say, six months, the whole matter was basically forgotten. I had re-signed the SAMs, I'd gone in to see my client again. It was resurrected with the war on terror. After 9/11, they needed bodies, they needed people.

MICHAEL RATNER: Let me go back for a second. The time when Fitzgerald called you and said, "Lynne, you violated SAMs," was what year?

STEWART: August 2000.

BOGHOSIAN: And violating a SAM, let's be perfectly clear, is not a criminal offense.

STEWART: It's not. It's interesting because people seem to think it's a court order or a crime. Actually, it is, as I said, it's a Bureau of Prisons regulation that they put in against the client and the lawyer merely signs on that they're aware of them. I don't want to minimize it, but I would say within the body of these rules and regulations, it said, "If you break these, you may be denied the right to visit your client." Just like so many prison regulations. Except in my case, they waited for two years and then they indicted and they didn't just indict, they said that it was materially aiding a terrorist organization.

RATNER: Now when they say they waited, we had a change in administrations, and we had 9/11, and then the current Bush administration and Ashcroft, who was attorney general, decided to look back at what had happened two years before.

SMITH: They wanted to make an example out of you and they wanted to scare lawyers. Ashcroft flies into New York and he gets on the David Letterman show and he announces that they've got this red-hot lawyer terrorist. What they had was a sixty-four-year-old grandmother, but they portrayed you as the devil, and when you dehumanize somebody like that, as we know, you're able to victimize them. They tried you in Lower Manhattan, they had a jury—

BOGHOSIAN: A few blocks away from the World Trade Center.

SMITH: Right near the hole. They had a jury, an anonymous jury that was escorted back and forth from their homes in a police van. I was at the trial. They had twenty-foot-high videos of Osama bin Laden—

STEWART: This is after the jury had been promised by the judge during the early questioning that Osama bin Laden had nothing to do with this because some of the jury said, "If it's Osama bin Laden, if he's in the case, I might have a problem with this." Then the judge said, "Oh, no. He's not in the case. He's got nothing to do with it." Yet, he did allow the government, pretty much out of box, to use these pictures, this videotape, that was found in the basement of my co-defendant.

SMITH: Yeah, and let's also say that they put you on trial with a translator and they also put you on trial with another fellow who was, perhaps, a Muslim, and had ties with people in Egypt and so on and he was doing stuff that you don't even know about, but in any case, they made an amalgam. They grouped you. They should have severed the trial, but they didn't, and they put you with other people, which made it much harder for you to defend yourself. They put on what was an eight-month trial, something like 17,000 pages of transcript.

STEWART: I would also say that one of the most remarkable things at the trial was that, in connection with Osama bin Laden and other pieces of evidence, the judge instructed the jury 750 times that they were to disregard this evidence as to Lynne Stewart, this was only introduced as to Mr. [Ahmed Abdel] Sattar, the third party that you mentioned, and that it was not offered for the truth in any case, but merely as to Mr. Sattar's state of mind. Here we have Osama parading, ten times his life size, across the courtroom on the individualized TV sets, and the judge telling them ignore this. Ignore this 750 times.

RATNER: The jury was out for a while, right?

STEWART: They were out for about a week. We know that there was some coercion. One of the black jurors came back a month after deliberations saying that she feared for her life in that jury room and felt she had to convict, but the judge basically brushed that aside. He said she could have come to me at any time. Not exactly true.

SMITH: And you were convicted.

STEWART: I was convicted of materially aiding a terrorist organization and conspiracy to materially aid—

RATNER: What was that? What kind of aid did you give them?

STEWART: Well, if you want to stretch this little thing out, it's really the theories of the government, and I appreciate you making a distinction between the Clinton government and the Bush administration; I don't see all that much distinction, but I must say, this Machiavellian government is beyond all belief; their theory was that I provided aid to the IG [the Egyptian Islamic Group], which is one of the listed terrorist organizations in Egyptian Islam.

By virtue of the fact that I brought the words of my client, I provided personal aid, by virtue of the words of the Sheikh [Omar Abdel Rahman] in the press release. That was their theory. That's the "materially aiding." This is a law that has been under attack. The judge in my case dismissed the first indictment, because he said, "Nobody, no lawyer, could know what the heck they were supposed to do."

BOGHOSIAN: The government then came back with a superseding indictment, essentially changing the definition of material support?

STEWART: No, they brought it under a different section of the law, which speaks in terms of knowledge and intent. The judge initially had said to us that he intended to charge knowledge and intent. Unfortunately, when we got down to the charge, he charged knowledge, but he didn't charge intent.

RATNER: They convicted you of having knowledge of providing these words, this press release, and what did the press release say?

STEWART: Well, it was more than that. Their contention is I knew who the Sheikh was. I had represented him from 1994. [Mohamed] Yousry knew who the Sheikh was, he was the subject of his Ph.D. thesis. The allegation was therefore that, knowing who the Sheikh was, and making the press release in light of this knowledge, indicated that we had knowledge that this was a terrorist and that it would be going to a terrorist organization.

RATNER: What did the press release say?

STEWART: Well, the press release, this is one of the great bones of contention here, the press release said, from the Sheikh, "Personally I no longer support a ceasefire that we unilaterally entered into."

That was the first press release and I can only say to you that it caused a tremendous furor because, of course, the IG was not expecting this and they didn't know how to cope with it. But it got a lot of press in the Middle East, got no press here whatsoever, but in the Middle East it caused a large furor and then we were asked to clarify it, at which point the Sheikh said again, "I'm not telling you to end the ceasefire. I am only saying to you that it does not appear from my vantage point, in the middle of Minnesota, to be working."

He's hearing about people being killed ex-officially. He's hearing about arrests, the tortures in the jails for which Egypt is famous. He said, "It doesn't appear to be working, so let's raise up the media attention and go forward, but this is for you to decide. You're there on the ground." I don't think he said "on the ground," that's a real Bushism, but anyway, they got this message. Now, the government wanted to say this was a directive from the chief of the IG to resume armed struggle, to start killing people again.

RATNER: In fact, the ceasefire never was lifted and nobody was hurt, were they?

STEWART: Exactly.

RATNER: They still, they want to send you, now a sixty-eight-year-old grandmother, to prison for thirty years.

STEWART: Yeah.

RATNER: And that's what it was all about when we were in the appellate court.

BOGHOSIAN: It was about the sentencing that the judge imposed and the government's argument was that you should get thirty years, rather than the two years and four months that he gave you.

RATNER: Right. Back at the district court, the government, as was said, asked for thirty years, and the judge, after getting a thousand letters in your support, after talking about what you've done in the bar, how you represent people with no money, everybody in your community—I've always been amazed by that when I go to your talks. There's a thousand people you've represented on everything from landlord-tenant, to small claims court, to major felonies. I mean, you're a major community and city and country resource and I think the judge recognized that. He basically gave you this twenty-eight-month sentence, which means you would do, based on parole—

STEWART: Probably. There's no parole in Feds anymore. Unfortunately or fortunately, whatever way you see the parole system, it's about a twenty-month sentence, maybe. It probably is unlikely. Because of the nature of what I'm convicted of.

RATNER: The government was not happy. When did that sentence come down?

STEWART: That was October 2006.

RATNER: It's over a year ago that you got sentenced. There's an appeal by the government saying the sentence is too short, and there's an appeal by you saying, "I was wrongfully convicted."

STEWART: I will say wrongfully convicted and you're familiar with briefs in the Second Circuit, they usually, if you send in a 101-page brief, they send it back to you, but we put in a 500-page brief.

RATNER: A 500-page brief. I'm going to use it to press leaves.

STEWART: One of the judges said, "We're well aware of the weight of your argument today." Held up these massive books. Judge Sack said, "I think Mr. [Joshua L.] Dratel," my lawyer, "I think every case in the English language you cited in your brief, so don't worry about it, we'll find it." At any rate, there were a million issues, as you know. There's a whole free speech issue, there's an issue of stretching the law, there's an issue of selective prosecution. My dear friend, Ramsey Clark, did the same exact things I did.

There's an issue of FISA [Foreign Intelligence Surveillance Act of 1978] and NSA wiretaps. We don't even know what happened there. We only know the judge decided against us when we raised it, but there were classified documents involved. I mean, there are a myriad of issues, issues, issues, but what we focused on yesterday was the intent and the knowledge issue and the First Amendment issue.

RATNER: The idea that you would need intent and knowledge to have materially aided a terrorist organization.

STEWART: Right. That you had to have both. That's our contention.

RATNER: Knowledge wouldn't be enough.

STEWART: Right, and that never did I have an intent. My intent was to serve my client. Not to serve his cause.

BOGHOSIAN: What is the First Amendment argument that Josh Dratel raised about?

STEWART: It's the fundamental love of the First Amendment lawyers and that is: yes, this is maybe reprehensible speech in some people's minds, but does not foretell imminent danger. It is nowhere near the standard set in *Brandenburg v. Ohio* [1969] or in *NAACP v. Claiborne Hardware Store* [1982], which was a black boycott of a hardware store in Mississippi, because it was a step removed and because nothing ever happened.

SMITH: Lynne, jumping over to the sentencing part: Why do you think Judge [John M.] Walker was so intent trying to restore that thirty-year sentence? To make an example out of you?

STEWART: The judge happens to be a first cousin of George Bush. We don't believe in bills of attainder. We're not saying he's guilty by reason of that, but right out of the first starting gate, the first questions he asked, he was making speeches about terrorism and Luxor and seventy people being killed. It's a very familiar government tactic to anybody that's done terrorism cases, where they make a great promulgation of the fear of terrorism, even if it has nothing to do with what we're talking about.

RATNER: Luxor, of course, is a big tourist site in Egypt where a number of American and other tourists were killed.

STEWART: Were killed in 1977. Long before this case.

RATNER: And of course, upper- and upper-middle-class, and middle-class people visit Luxor. So, I'm sure that Judge Walker was very concerned by this.

SMITH: We're going to keep track of everything that happens to you, Lynne, and we're here expressing, on behalf of our entire audience, our solidarity with you, our support, our love and good luck on this decision. I'm certainly confident on a good part of this decision.

STEWART: I'm feeling that I'm going to, as I have from day one, hope for the best and be ready, understanding politically where the country is at, be able to deal with the worst.

Lynne Stewart was interviewed on Law and Disorder *on October 20, 2008, by Heidi Boghosian, Michael Ratner, and Michael Steven Smith. This interview has been edited and condensed.*

MARGARET RATNER KUNSTLER

Margaret Ratner Kunstler (b. 1945) is a New York-based civil rights attorney. She was the educational director at the Center for Constitutional Rights where she originated the Movement Support Network. She authored If An Agent Knocks.

Most recently she co-authored, with Michael Ratner, the book Hell No: Your Right to Dissent in Twenty-First Century America.

She currently represents Julian Assange of WikiLeaks.

MARGARET RATNER KUNTSLER: I was a red diaper baby, in that my parents were active in the Communist Party, but they were also always very secretive about it, very nervous and scared. I was taught to keep secrets. I didn't even know what the secrets were, but I couldn't reveal anything; everything was a secret. I think they were afraid of being subpoenaed. One morning I woke up, and the entire library had disappeared. I know that there were people who responded much more courageously to the Red Scare than my parents did. They just were not capable of that kind of strength.

The overall effect of all this was to make me an introvert. I was always afraid to say anything. By high school, when I wanted finally to go on demonstrations, it was a battle. They didn't want me participating in any political activity. I would say, "Mommy, everybody is on the bus. Why can't I be on the bus?" A couple of times they let me go on the bus, though they were still very nervous. When I went away to college, I had more freedom—and then, I did get on the bus at every opportunity.

I didn't go to law school initially. I went to the Institute of Fine Arts at NYU, to study art history. I had a great fellowship. But at the end of my first year, I decided not to continue. There were a couple of things about it that really upset me. For example, every Friday, they had a tea, where one of the female students had to serve the tea. I refused to pour tea, and I never went to their teas. Also, the students were very stiff. They wouldn't share ideas, because they were writing them up. These attitudes made me feel funny; I didn't want to have to live with them for all the years it would take until I could get a job. So I applied instead to law school at Columbia, where I was accepted.

Columbia University in the '60s, though the scene of the great student riots, was very active in supporting the [Vietnam] war. Many of its departments were working together with the Intelligence Services. Research has been done on Columbia's then racism. At the same time, they were building a gym in Morningside Park, one of the few public parks in Harlem. We were all frustrated about the war. We couldn't get anywhere in terms of stopping it—there were mass demonstrations all the time. I met a lot of wonderful people. The law school was not as active as the university, though a number of law students did occupy buildings. Most of us, however, just picketed and did other things.

After seven hundred people were arrested at Columbia on April 30, 1968, we figured we needed a response, and also needed to figure out how to represent so many people. That is when Columbia's chapter of the National Lawyers Guild, which hadn't been active since the '50s because of the Red Scare, re-formed. We brought a lawsuit against the university, outlining all the issues the students were trying to bring to attention. A number of us in the NLG office worked getting lawyers to represent the seven hundred who were arrested. I spent the summer of 1968 that way, finding lawyers and going to court occasionally. This was the beginning of the Mass Defense Committee, which still continues to this day.

My first job after graduating was with the criminal division of NYC Legal Aid. I seem to have said something objectionable to them, so I was sent to Brooklyn, at the same time as the great liberal African American judge Bruce Wright was punished the same way. We were exiled to Brooklyn together, you could say. We had a wonderful time trying misdemeanors like possession of stolen vehicles. I tried and Bruce acquitted every one of those cases. The defense was always, "I bought it at the barbershop." Now, most people don't know how central a barbershop was to the black community at that time. Business deals were conducted there. So, Bruce of course understood that.

I also did some private practice with Michael Ratner, in a wonderful building at 351 Broadway that still exists. We did a lot of interesting work. I also did work for the Grand Jury Project with the NLG. In those days, federal grand juries were subpoenaing people whom they believed to be political activists. You had to talk or risk being jailed.

We did a book advising lawyers how to represent witnesses before federal grand juries. You would get them to refuse to testify, and then they would be given immunity. In 1966, they limited the Immunity Law to just the things you specifically testified to at the time. This meant that if you were subpoenaed to the grand jury and refused to testify, the U.S. attorney could go to the Justice Department in Washington and get an immunity order. Then if you still refused to testify, you got a contempt hearing, and could get jail time. Many people spent months in jail because of this.

I worked for the Center for Constitutional Rights during the Central American wars. I was advising people all over the country what to do if an FBI agent came to visit them, writing a pamphlet called *If An Agent Knocks*. And it wasn't just visits, it was traveling to Cuba, sending medicine to Cuba, traveling to Nicaragua. At that time, they were really black bag jobs, where the FBI broke into various offices, including the Center's. I went back to mass defense at that point. In 2004, during the Republican National Convention in New York, where a huge number of people were preemptively arrested, I led the writ squad. We had expected that there would be a lot of demonstrating around it. About six months beforehand, we formed different squads to deal with the arrests and everything else that was most likely going to happen: a squad for getting permits, one for writ of habeas corpus, one for getting to lawyers to get people out of jail. The writ squad was for if people were held for over twenty-four hours. In fact, it was successful and did get damages, which we then contributed to the Guild. People were being detained in horrible conditions, and the judge made an example of the prosecution in that case. It was very dramatic. The Guild did a great job. It was all the advance planning that made it possible.

Throughout all this, I was raising two daughters, Sarah and Emily Kunstler, now both wonderfully accomplished in their own right. At first, it was easier, because there were so many people in the movement who were volunteering to help in any way. When I would go to federal court, when I was breastfeeding, there would always be someone to carry Sarah into the court.

Later, when the movement wasn't as strong, it became more difficult. Fortunately for me, my mother then stepped in when they were around eight years old to take care of them. I called her my "Great Emancipator."

I married Bill Kunstler, the civil rights lawyer, whom I met at the Center for Constitutional Rights. He wasn't on staff, but he had an office there. He was always looking for someone to second-chair him in cases. Since I really wanted to be a criminal defense attorney, I jumped at the opportunity. The first case I did with him was not a criminal case, though. It was a civil case where a large group of people had gone to a political meeting and the police had busted it up and arrested everybody for no reason at all. We expunged their records, and that was the first trial I ever had with him. The second case was in Norfolk, Virginia, where every year they have an Azalea Festival. Our client had been accused of throwing a rock at the Azalea Queen. When

Bill cross-examined the cop, he asked him which hand he threw the rock with. The cop said, "The right one." Then, when the client took the stand, he asked him if he was right- or left-handed, and he threw a ball to him. And so he was acquitted. We've all heard this story before, but it's so rare that it would work.

I was also one of the lawyers on the Attica case, on the only conviction.

And I did work with Anonymous—a loose association of hackers who do various hacking or Internet activities to support political causes that they agree with. I put the word out that if any Anonymous-related cases came up in New York City, I would like to know about it. I got a call from a lawyer in Chicago saying that a client whom I had represented the previous year, on an assault charge for a battle with some Neo-Nazis, was being transferred to New York on a federal charge related to hacking. I wanted to take the case, but needed some institutional support. I got Elizabeth Fink from the federal judge–approved Criminal Justice Act panel of attorneys, and we got the case.

Right now I'm representing Sarah Harrison, who accompanied Edward Snowden to Hong Kong. She released a statement that I thought was so brave and bold, explaining why she had done what she did. I sent it to my daughters. It was on the level of Anita Hill, these tremendously heroic women who stand up and do very scary things.

I wrote to Sarah and let her know—I said that the statement was so beautiful and that I loved it, and that if she ever needed help I would be available. Our feeling was that she would not be tried separately, but that if either Snowden or Julian Assange went to trial, she would be tried as a co-conspirator. I investigated and got her a lawyer in London whom she likes very much. She's British but she's in a community of ex-pats in Berlin, because it's safer to be in Berlin than in London.

I don't believe that rule of law and democracy are compatible with capitalism. As long as the means of production are not in the hands of the people who do the work, there will be injustice and inequality in the world.

My advice to young lawyers? It's important to take a risk. It's critically important to get involved anywhere in the country you see something happening, and travel there if possible—years ago, we would travel to Wounded Knee, or wherever, so easily. I recommend we bring back the itinerant lawyer, and get to work.

Margaret Ratner Kunstler was interviewed on Law and Disorder *on July 4, 2016, by Michael Steven Smith and Heidi Boghosian. This interview has been edited and condensed.*

ABDEEN JABARA

Michigan-born Abdeen Jabara (b. 1940) is a New York City-based civil rights attorney and co-founder of the American-Arab Anti-Discrimination Committee.

As a young attorney in Detroit in 1960, he became a supporter of Palestinian resistance to Zionist colonialism and is a central figure in the National Lawyers Guild in this regard.

ABDEEN JABARA: I grew up in an ethnic family in a small town in northern Michigan. My parents had both immigrated there from Lebanon. My maternal grandfather had actually come to North Dakota in the latter part of the nineteenth century, and homesteaded there. His first daughter, my mother, was born in Lebanon, and came over as a three-year-old along with my grandmother, in 1906. She married my father in 1923 in Minneapolis. They settled in this small town where my father had a grocery business, and raised a family of seven children, of which I was the youngest.

We were one of two Arab families in the town. At the time, we thought of ourselves as Syrian. My family was in the grocery business, and I worked in the store. My father was killed in an automobile accident. I was ten years old. That had a very traumatic impact on me. I really didn't know him as an adult. I remember he had a very strong ethnic identity. He was not afraid to speak Arabic to my older siblings in front of customers in the store, although they cringed when he did that. When people asked him, "Where are you from?"

he would sometimes draw a map of the Middle East on a carton, or one of the boxes, and show it to them.

I also have a memory of him leaning down to listen to the shortwave radio in 1948. I would have been eight years old. He was listening to some Arabic radio program, which I didn't understand at the time, and only later on did I figure out that what he was following was the incredible turmoil that was happening in Palestine.

Well, I went on working in our family store, and when I finished high school, I went away to the University of Michigan. There were thirty-four in my graduating class. They had a language requirement. They said, "You've got to take some foreign language." So, I said, "I'll take Arabic." Even though I really knew maybe a hundred words in Arabic, some of which were cuss words.

MICHAEL STEVEN SMITH: It's like me and Margaret with Yiddish.

JABARA: So I study Arabic for two years, and I then I decided, "Well, I'm not gonna learn it this way. I'm gonna do some immersion tactics." I just pulled up and went to Egypt, where I lived with the family of my sister's husband. I spent six months there, and it really was quite a culture shock, after being in this small town in Ann Arbor, Michigan, and then going to Egypt and finding poverty and all those problems. It was during the period of Arab Nationalism, and Nasser was in power at the time. After spending six months there, I traveled to Lebanon for my first visit. I visited both my mother's and my father's villages, and then went up to Aleppo and took the Orient Express all the way back to England, and then I returned to the U.S. to finish my undergrad. I was taking pre-legal studies. Then I went on to law school at Wayne State University.

This was the time of the civil rights movement and the anti-Vietnam War movement. But the law school students were very conservative. I started a chapter of the Law Students' Civil Rights Research Council and we brought Malcom X and Herbert Aptheker to speak. This was way out for the law school. It was an incredible experience.

I clerked for Ernest Goodman, who was trying to revive the National Lawyers Guild after it had been decimated by the McCarthy period. They were sending lawyers down to the South to work in the civil rights movement.

After taking the bar exam, I was totally wiped out. I said, "To hell with it. I don't want to go to work. I don't want to get involved in the rat race." I spent four months at an Arabic language school in Lebanon, but then the tuition was too high, so I went down to Beirut and worked for the Palestinian Research Center. I wrote a monograph about the Egyptian–Israeli Armistice Agreement. Beirut at the time had a *la dolce vita* atmosphere. It was called the Switzerland of the Middle East.

Being there was an incredible experience. But after I finished that, I couldn't find any other employment. I didn't want to go back to the United States. I made my way to Paris, where I tried to find a job, but I couldn't—so I came and opened my solo law practice in Detroit, because they had a fairly large Arab community, though it wasn't nearly as large then as it is today. I thought I could get some clients there because of my speaking Arabic. I'd learned how to handle personal injury cases, and I thought I would use that as the basis for my work. Shortly after this, the 1967 Arab–Israeli war broke out. And there was this huge uprising of the Detroit black population that same year. Both of these were incredible events that I experienced just as I was starting out there.

I was secretary of the Lawyers Guild chapter in Detroit. Two of the members of the Lawyers Guild called a special meeting, not to discuss the burning and the police violence in Detroit but to have the Lawyers Guild send letters to the Soviet Union to protest their supplying arms to the Arab countries. They wanted to expel me from the Lawyers Guild, these two members, I will never forget. They had their special meeting. Bill Goodman, now a dear friend, defended me and, of course, I was not expelled. Those two actually withdrew from the Lawyers Guild. One of them was Bernie Fieger, the father of the famous attorney in Detroit [Geoffrey Fieger], who had nothing to do with the Lawyers Guild.

Following that, there was a meeting of the International Oriental Society at the University of Michigan in Ann Arbor, and one of the professors there invited me to attend. The people who attended this meeting were all Arabic professors at different universities in the U.S., and they were totally devastated. They said, "What can we do? This is terrible!"

That is when my first organizing effort in the Arab American community started. It was with the creation of the Association of Arab-American University Graduates [AAUG], which from 1968 until the creation of the American-Arab Anti-Discrimination Committee [ADC] in 1980 was the principal national Arab American organization. The AAUG was still restricted to university graduates and it was very academic in its approach, holding these conferences and bringing in eminent speakers from overseas. I was the original founding secretary, and I served as its president in 1972.

The American administration had been supplying weaponry to Israel way before the '67 war. The principal suppliers were France and Britain, and the United States started supplying them in 1965. Then the Johnson administration gave Israel the green light for the '67 war, in which they occupied portions of Egypt, parts of Syria, and the remainder of Palestine and the West Bank, which had been part of Jordan because of some collusion between the Hashemite Monarchy and Israel in 1948.

This was an incredibly devastating situation. Our response was to start organizing ourselves, in order to have at least some degree of protection and sanity amidst the madness in the U.S., because the American press and the politicians were trumpeting the defeat of the Arabs as an American victory.

It was amazing. Gerald Ford said, "Israel is our battleship in the Middle East." And of course, the U.S. had been helping to fund the whole settlement process inside of Israel through the tax-exempt status of the United Israel Appeal and the United Jewish Appeal.

After '67, the United States became Israel's principal backer. But at the same time, there began to develop a real, genuine, mass popular Palestinian resistance, with the rise of the Palestinian Liberation Organization. All kinds of reports were coming out about Israeli practices—torture, land confiscations, kicking people out of their homes. So, in 1969, I submitted a resolution to the National Lawyers Guild about Israel's violations of the four Geneva conventions. The head of the resolutions committee, whose name I will not mention, said, "Well, we don't know enough about this. We had better table this resolution, and you write an article for the *Guild Notes* about this subject." I wrote the article and submitted it, and it didn't get published. When I asked them, "Why didn't you publish this article?" they said they were trying to find somebody to write a rebuttal to it. They finally published the article without a rebuttal, but with a note by the editor, who was president of the Guild at the time, that was a disclaimer about any Guild connection to the article.

SMITH: The narrative at that time, which was widely believed, was that Israel was merely defending itself, even as it was grabbing land in three directions. And that was what you were up against.

JABARA: Then, in 1972, when I was president of the AAUG, the U.S. government announced something called Operation Boulder. This was an interdepartmental, inter-agency effort to screen all activists on the Palestinian issue in the U.S., to screen all Arab-surnamed visa applicants before being granted visas to come to the U.S., and to screen all Arab students on campuses.

They were working hand-in-glove with the Anti-Defamation League (ADL), which had been surveilling pro-Palestinian activity in the U.S. for a long time. And the ADL was supplying information to the FBI. They claimed they were a civil rights organization, but in point of fact they ran this spying operation in the U.S., which finally came to light in 1993, when they were exposed by the FBI. They were also spying on anti-Apartheid activists in South Africa, because of the alliance between Israel and South Africa. It was incredible. We published a small piece in the Sunday *New York Times* about how the Nixon administration announced Operation Boulder, playing politics with civil liberties. We got called in for an audit on our tax-exempt status because of that. In the meantime, I was collecting all these affidavits from all these young Palestinians all over the country who were being hauled in for immigration-deportation hearings. I was just overwhelmed with this work, because there weren't a lot of attorneys who were doing work in this area.

We got some political support. Phil Hart, a senator in Michigan, wrote a very strong letter condemning this dragnet operation by the Nixon administration. We continued not to have much impact, because at the time it was "The Arab was the terrorist." It wasn't "the Muslim," it was "the Arab," right? It was people like Jeane Kirkpatrick, U.S. representative to the UN, who were saying that the terrorist movement was something that was generated by the Soviet Union, if you recall, at the time. They were pushing this whole business about the Soviet Union being connected with terrorism, and that the PLO was a terrorist organization, etc. This is what we had to face. We were living in a situation where Arabs were being demonized. It got so bad that in the late '70s, William Webster, the director of the FBI, created something called ABSCAM. ABSCAM was an operation where they dressed up a couple of FBI employees, Italian-Americans, with Arab headdresses, to look like they were Arabs, to entrap certain congressmen who were on the take. They got it on film, and showed it on the news all the time.

At that point in time, my wonderful friend and colleague Jim Abourezk was like a godsend. He came out of South Dakota, this small state, and he was a huge defender of Native American rights. He was part of a real populist movement in South Dakota. He had been a member of the House, and he became a senator, and served one term in the Senate. I first met him when he came to Detroit for a fundraiser we had for him when he was running for the Senate. And he got into the Senate. Then he quit. They had attacked his son, Charlie, trying to find some dirt on him. So he quit the Senate and he came to Detroit and agreed to help start this organization [the ADC]. He was fearless. There had been other Arab Americans in Congress, but none of them would touch this whole issue with a ten-foot pole. He came and started this organization [the ADC], which I was on the board of, and then became vice chairman. I ultimately resigned from my law practice, closed my law office, and moved to Washington to become president of the organization. I did that for four years. It was like hitting my head against the proverbial wall, but I thought that if we could organize this community, they could have some kind of influence. And we did. We made a big impact on the stereotyping issue. We were able to win battles on that. We came in the footsteps of the civil rights movement in that regard.

I had two people that I developed a relationship with in Detroit during the years I was practicing there—one was George Crockett, an African American congressman from Detroit, and the other was John Conyers, also a congressman. We got Arab Americans working on their staff. When they went to Washington we were able to work with them to some extent, but they didn't have that much power. The Black Caucus didn't have that much power either, but they gave us what help they could. John Conyers called some hearings about the attacks that were happening on Arab Americans all over the country, on ADC offices—the assassination of our West Coast regional director, Alex Odeh, the bombing of our office in Massachusetts, and the attack on our representative in New York. John Conyers held hearings on these, and then when George Crockett came to Washington he was a stalwart. He was absolutely wonderful. I remember during the First Intifada, he was a member of the House Foreign Affairs Committee, and he called me up. He said, "You know, they're not going to do anything in the Foreign Affairs Committee, but if you get me some witnesses, I'll set up a room in the House office building and we'll have unofficial hearings. We'll put out a press release about it." Which he did. He did what he could do. He knew what the game was in Washington, and I'll tell you, he was one of the most courageous and wonderful people that I have ever met.

SMITH: Didn't he have a National Lawyers Guild flag up in his office in Congress?

JABARA: Yes, he was a member, as was John Conyers—both were members of the National Lawyers Guild.

MARGARET RATNER KUNSTLER: Did this develop into some form of litigation that you participated in?

JABARA: I've been involved in a lot of litigation over the years, but as our recently deceased colleague Liz Fink once said, "There's no justice in America, only the struggle for justice." I have a very jaundiced view of the value of litigation in achieving justice. So my whole political work has been to intersect with other mass movements that were happening—the peace movement, the anti-war movement, the civil rights movement, the gay and lesbian movement, all of these different movements—because I thought there was an intersection in the struggle for peace and justice with all of these movements, and that all of us working together would have much more impact than us working separately. But I did get involved in lawsuits. One of the lawsuits was when I was with ADC. We found out that AIPAC—the American Israel Public Affairs Committee—was violating provisions of the Federal Election Campaign Act. AIPAC is the principal Israeli or Zionist lobby in the U.S., incredibly powerful and with a huge budget and a huge lobbying arm. We found out that they had set up a whole host of these individual PACs [Political Action Committees] all over the country, with non-descript names, that were giving the maximum. They would target somebody and have all these PACs give money to the candidates.

SMITH: They were able to target people and get them defeated.

JABARA: Exactly. We did a lot of research, studied a lot of reports, and I had a helluva time finding a lawyer that would take the case. We finally got the case, and we went to district court, where we lost, and then Dan Schember, another Lawyers Guild attorney, and I asked for an en banc hearing, and we won it. It was unheard of; I couldn't believe it. But there was one judge who was highly respected on that bench who understood what was happening, so he ruled in our favor. The Federal Election Commission was, you know, an old boys' club for the Democrat and Republican Parties. They go after small violators, but not the big ones. So the Federal Election Commission appealed to the Supreme Court, and it was at that point, and only at that point, that AIPAC filed an amicus brief; and what did the Supreme Court do? They remanded the case back to the Federal Election Commission. Which, of course, was the source of the problem! There were other cases I was involved in—we tried to challenge the tax-exempt status given to the United Jewish Appeal and the United Israel Appeal. That's a whole other long story. And a lot of my time was basically spent trying to do basic defense work for people in the movement who were being harassed.

RATNER: Your interest in joining the Arab American movement and all of those other movements developed historically into your work in the National Lawyers Guild, did it not?

JABARA: Yes, I think both of them actually went side by side. In 1977, I led the first delegation of the Lawyers Guild to the Middle East. That was after the Guild had adopted eight questions that all the chapters around the country were supposed to study. They were fantastic questions: Were the Palestinians entitled to self-determination? Were the Jews entitled to self-determination? Are the Palestinians entitled to Right of Return? All of these questions were posited by the National Executive Committee for different chapters to study, and they held studies around the country. It was incredible.

So after that was done, I took this delegation over, and we traveled to Lebanon, Syria, Jordan, and the West Bank and Gaza.

We were ten members, four of whom were Jewish. One of them turned out to be an arch-Zionist. He had written a letter to his girlfriend with all the information about where we had been, whom we had visited—we had seen Arafat in Beirut—and the Israelis found it. They singled out four of us for a strip search, three Jews and me. My goodness, what an experience that was. We were on the go, meeting and talking to people, torture victims; the stories we heard were incredible. We came back just at the time that the Lawyers Guild convention was being held in Seattle, Washington. We were all hyped up from the trip, and we go to this convention with two resolutions, a political one and a human rights one. Two of the chapters in the Guild were opposed to any kind of Guild action on these resolutions. And there was one individual, a very respected member of the Guild, who'd been there for many years, who intervened, and became a kind of go-between between these two chapters and our delegation. We worked out a compromise on a political resolution, which passed, but some people still were not happy. And people left the Guild because of that. Alan Dershowitz wrote a scathing attack on the Guild in the *American Lawyer*, because someone from the Guild had gone to him and told him what had happened. Then at the next executive committee meeting, they brought up the issue of the human rights resolution, which was a big sticking point because we had put in there "the systematic use of torture in the interrogation of Palestinians." Well, there was a huge fight-back on the use of the word, "systematic." So again, this one individual here in New York, who was acting as a go-between, came in, and we came up with some language—"numerous instances" or something like that—to try and placate these opponents that denied that Israel could be using systematic torture in the interrogation of Palestinian suspects.

There have been many Guild delegations, and many reports since that time—and I can't tell you, the respect I have for this organization. It really dealt in the most principled fashion, even though it lost money because of it, even though it lost members. But you have to remember, I came into this work in the Guild at a time when it was changing radically. The New Left was coming in, young lawyers that had come up in the movement and were more conscious of the anti-war movement and about American imperialism and American involvement overseas, and they made connections in a way that the old-time Lawyers Guild had not.

RATNER: Could you tell us about the time you got arrested?

JABARA: I was head of the ADC at the time. I was in Washington, and the Israelis announced in '87 that they were closing off all the entrances to Gaza and not allowing any foodstuffs in. We had to do something dramatic. I had the staff get some big, twenty-five-pound, fifty-pound bags of flour and sugar, and we said, "We're gonna go and we're gonna dump this right on the doorstep of the Israeli Embassy in Washington." Well, there was a law in Washington that you couldn't demonstrate within one hundred feet of any embassy.

So I got four other people who were heads of organizations to join me, and we drove up and took these bags out of the trunk. There were these buses that were lined up out there. The press was there. They had gotten word that we were gonna do this. They must have figured we would have a lot more people there. We didn't, we just wanted to make a statement. So we went up and put these bags there, and got arrested, and taken down and charged.

And ultimately the whole ordinance got struck down, so we got our records cleared. That's the only time I got arrested.

When I was with the ADC we were always trying to counteract our powerlessness. We were a very small organization with a very small amount of funding. For instance, when we learned that the Israeli general who had overseen the Sabra and Shatila massacres in Beirut had been appointed Israeli military attaché, we were outraged that the U.S. would allow this war criminal to come to Washington. We found out where he lived. We held demonstrations there. We brought a lawsuit against him. We got his photograph and put it up in subway cars with a quote from the Israeli commission that investigated the massacres. Ultimately, he was withdrawn from Washington, and got some other high position in Israel.

So we tried with our limited resources to find creative ways to highlight these different issues. It was not an easy task, and I basically got burned out trying to do it, but it was an interesting experience and I'm not sorry that I undertook it.

RATNER: What do you notice about how things are different today than they were when you began this?

JABARA: There's an enormous difference. So many Jewish Americans are now questioning what Israel is doing, and questioning what Zionism is. I think those are really important factors. There's no longer this unified position in which AIPAC is the only force out there. We've got organizations like Jewish Voice for Peace that do marvelous work, and I think it's cumulative, and it's all having an important impact. And I'm optimistic, because you can't be involved in this work unless you retain optimism. You have to believe that change is possible, and that's what I believe in.

Abdeen Jabara was interviewed on Law and Disorder *on January 11, 2016, by Michael Steven Smith and Margaret Ratner Kunstler. This interview has been edited and condensed.*

CHARLES ABOUREZK

Charles Abourezk (b. 1953) is a partner in the Abourezk Law Firm in Rapid City, South Dakota. He is a trial attorney, author, filmmaker, and the chief justice of the Rosebud Sioux Tribe Supreme Court. He has served as a member of the South Dakota Advisory Committee to the United States Commission on Civil Rights. Abourezk's documentary, A Tattoo on My Heart: The Warriors of Wounded Knee 1973, *tells the story of the men and women involved in the siege.*

HEIDI BOGHOSIAN: We understand you're chief justice of the Rosebud Sioux Tribe Supreme Court.

CHARLES ABOUREZK: The Rosebud Sioux Tribe is the second largest tribe in South Dakota. There are nine tribal governments total in the state. It's the state where I grew up. I spent much of my adult life over in the Pine Ridge Reservation, which has been for a number of years the poorest county in the United States, and I work in both places.

BOGHOSIAN: How did you get interested in the law?

ABOUREZK: It grew out of my community organization work in Pine Ridge back in the '70s.

There was, at the time, a heavy FBI presence on the Pine Ridge Reservation. I served the purpose of assisting individuals by advising them of their constitutional rights, and I became interested in the law, and eventually went back later in life to law school to become a tribally licensed lawyer. This was long after I had worked for a number of Indian organizations, including a Native American NGO that worked at the UN. I worked there for a number of years on human rights issues for Indians from the Americas.

The Pine Ridge Reservation is the second largest reservation in the United States. It's located in southwestern South Dakota. It's a huge land mass. It takes about an hour and a half to drive diagonally across the reservation. There's very little economy there. The geography is poor. It lends itself to some cattle grazing, but not much in terms of raising crops.

MICHAEL RATNER: You said you were out there in the '70s at Pine Ridge, and I know that's the period when Wounded Knee happened. Were you around then?

ABOUREZK: No, I had gone out and was living in Virginia for a short while. I returned at the end of 1973, and went down to help with the election campaign in '74 against Dick Wilson, the former tribal chairman, who many had felt had been repressive, particularly toward traditional people on the reservation. He was aligned with the U.S. government and the FBI. So that's how I got re-introduced to the Pine Ridge Reservation.

RATNER: I know you made a movie called *A Tattoo on My Heart: The Warriors of Wounded Knee 1973.*

ABOUREZK: Wounded Knee was the site of the 1890 massacre in which almost three hundred American Indians from several different tribes were killed by the U.S. Army. They were surrounded and, essentially, murdered on that spot. By the 1970s, there had been a lot of racial discrimination and some racially motivated killings of Indian people, and in 1973 the American Indian movement returned and joined forces with the traditional people who had long been neglected on the reservation. They decided to engage in a protest—and they chose the site of the massacre at Wounded Knee to stage that protest.

They set up a line there. The government, the FBI, and the U.S. Marshals, along with Dick Wilson's followers who were armed and called "the goon squad," formed the other side of that line. The siege lasted seventy-one days.

It was finally dismantled, and a number of people were prosecuted and so on as a result of that.

At Wounded Knee, there were two Indian people killed, and one marshal wounded. The first fatality was Frank Clearwater. He was a medic who had just arrived within a few days, and he was shot in the head by a federal round as he was in the basement of the church there. The second was Buddy Lamont, who had been serving in the U.S. Army in Vietnam, and had come back and decided to go AWOL and fight for his people instead. Buddy was killed at about a thousand yards with a fairly large round. I think they said it was a .300 or something like that. Shot right in the chest. I think that was the beginning of the end of the protest, because that had been such a stark and overt killing of an Indian person, and they began to start to negotiate at that point.

BOGHOSIAN: Charlie, tell us about your film, *A Tattoo on My Heart,* and what motivated you to make it. What did you intend to do with it?

ABOUREZK: I realized that a lot of people who were involved in Wounded Knee, many of whom I'd known over the years, were starting to pass away, and I thought their stories needed to be documented. I set to work and a friend of mine, Brett Lawler, agreed to co-produce and co-direct it with me. On the thirtieth anniversary of Wounded Knee, we set up a recording studio right at the Wounded Knee School, and just took people's stories. I did the interviews. They're very powerful.

There are some stories that didn't really fit with the arc of the film, but which were incredibly powerful, and I'm glad I documented them, because seven or eight of the people who were in the documentary have now passed away. We're happy that we were able to freeze that moment in time and get those stories down.

BOGHOSIAN: Can you tell us about one or two other cases that you've worked on within the Native American community that have been important to you?

ABOUREZK: I continued to be a strong advocate for tribal sovereignty and self-determination and the rights of individual Indians, especially within the dynamic of racial discrimination, which at times in South Dakota has been as bad as the South is toward African Americans. There's been some improvement in the last ten years or so, but you still see incidents of racial discrimination. I helped a firm to preserve the boundaries of the ancient Sioux reservation; that went up to the U.S. Supreme Court twice, and I was the lead counsel, and we were finally able to win that one.

One of my favorite cases is that of a Native American man from Rosebud, who was out shopping with his family. He's a sun dancer, he doesn't drink. While his family was at the grocery store, he went over to the liquor store. His mother was from Puerto Rico; his father was Native American. She had passed away, and he used to buy one bottle of rum a year, and pour one drink out on her grave once a month to remember her.

He went in to order that annual bottle, wearing an army jacket, and the lady refused to sell him the rum. She said, "You're drunk," and he says, "No I'm not, I don't drink." Then he says, "Well, can I at least buy these other items?" She says, "No, I'm not selling you anything." He says, "Well, can I speak to the manager?" and she started yelling for security. Three guys came over. They roughed him up inside the store, took him outside, and from a standing position slammed him face down onto the pavement. Then they called the police, and the police came and arrested him, and took him to jail. In that process, while he was face down, one of the store employees put their knee in his back and wrenched him up backward, and ruptured a disc in his lower back.

We went to trial on that with an all-white jury. We were able to prevail and get a $212,000 verdict, and that made a lot of Indian people in the area feel good, because it reflected the treatment that they often received in the commercial sector around here.

RATNER: You are a Supreme Court judge for the Rosebud Sioux Tribe, and you're also a practicing lawyer at the same time?

ABOUREZK: I was a Supreme Court Justice on the Pine Ridge Reservation for their Supreme Court, and I retired from that position. I continue to be a trial lawyer, and still represent many tribal schools, tribal organizations, and Indian tribes.

Many people don't realize that, except for limited jurisdiction that the federal government has on criminal matters, the civil jurisdiction for incidents which occur within the reservation lies with the tribal court, as do criminal misdemeanors, both for Indians and non-member Indians, meaning Indians from other tribes that happen to be living on the reservation.

They used to have criminal jurisdiction over whites until 1978, when Justice Rehnquist, in a case called *Oliphant*, reversed that, and would not allow them to have criminal jurisdiction over whites anymore. These are functioning courts. At the Rosebud lower court, all the judges are law-trained. It's actually quite a wonderful court to try cases in.

These courts are very modern, but they also try to reflect traditional notions of justice; many courts have a traditional mediation diversion program, so they can refer people to elders and let them work out conflicts. This is a good thing, because in the Native American view, you can't really have winners and losers. You have to restore the harmony or the balance within the tribe.

BOGHOSIAN: We wanted to talk briefly about your father, James George Abourezk, who's a former Democratic U.S. representative and U.S. senator who was critical of U.S. foreign policy in Israel and Palestine. Can you speak briefly about how that case of colonialism relates to what you see in Native American communities in South Dakota, for example?

ABOUREZK: I know that's a sensitive issue, but the American government adopted a British style of colonialism, as did the Israelis when they began to colonize parts of Palestine. You see, it goes in four steps: first, the disruption of traditional agriculture and food gathering, which out here was done in two ways. One by killing off the buffalo, and secondly by constraining them from moving around in a wide arc, and hunting and gathering in different parts of the country, by putting them on the reservation.

The second thing was to transfer commonly owned land into private ownership, to turn land into a commodity that could be bought and sold, and they did that through what was called the Dawes Act, or the Allotment Act in the late 1800s. That's actually an act that President Theodore Roosevelt, in one of his addresses in early 1900s, called, "a mighty pulverizing machine with which to break up the tribal mass." That was a deliberate act to isolate and reduce the land areas of the American Indians.

The third step was to develop a Native American ruling elite, the so-called "paper chiefs." In the 1930s, this grew into modern tribal government, which was loosely modeled on the American system except that the Department of the Interior sent out constitutions without a separation of powers, which remain in effect in most reservations today. The lack of separation of powers was by government design.

The last step was to develop an educated elite, and of course, as with any colonizing project anywhere, that's the step that always backfires. Because when people get sent off to the mother country or to get educated, they become most acutely aware of the oppression of their people. That happened with the Indians in the relocation era in the 1950s. Indians were sent to the cities to learn how to be good factory workers and so on, and learn trades and skills, and it was a one-way ticket.

You didn't get a ticket back home, and so many people ended up there, and raised their children in places like San Francisco, L.A., Chicago, and Minneapolis. When the era of activism among Indians happened in the early 1970s, that's where they came from. The children of those relocated people from that program became the American Indian movement; they were the ones who came back home and joined forces with the traditional people, standing up against racism and in favor of tribal sovereignty and self-determination.

So you see many parallels between that and what's happening with the Palestinians in the West Bank and Gaza.

RATNER: You spend a lot of time, obviously, in South Dakota, on at least two reservations. Have you seen any evolution in terms of better treatment, better economic situation? We always read about Pine Ridge, and the dislocations there, the poverty, et cetera. What's it like now?

ABOUREZK: The one thing I want to clear up right away is that there's a general perception in the United States that all tribes have really good Indian gaming, and therefore the government doesn't have to fulfill its obligations. And that's far from true. Other than California, which has a huge population base, there's probably only two other areas where gaming is really successful, and that's in the Minneapolis area (Shakopee) and in Connecticut. Other than that, tribes have a very low base; even if they have a casino, they really aren't making it. That's true of Pine Ridge and other reservations. It's mostly utilized by tribal members.

You still see huge unemployment, huge economic problems, and all the social problems that flow from that. I was on the Pine Ridge Reservation when Reagan came into office, and unemployment was at 35 percent. When he left office, and after he'd killed off a number of federal programs, unemployment was at 85 percent. So we saw a marked and very clear change in the situation of people who were really pushed to the fringes of American society, as a result of Reagan-era programs or lack thereof, and they've never really recovered from that.

I would say that most reservations in the United States, other than those very few that have successful gaming, still need the kind of commitment of a Marshall Plan, or some kind of a reconstruction like we saw in Europe after World War II with Germany and Japan. We never did that for Indians, and we still owe them that, because after all, we occupied and took most of their lands.

I would point you to the work of Dr. William Julius Wilson, who, when he was in Chicago, did a study there and showed that the problems in the black community did not come from some sort of disintegration in black families, as Senator Moynihan suggested, but were the result of corporations leaving the inner cities and fleeing to third world countries where they could make more profits.

Wealth has no loyalty, and as a result, as Dr. Wilson said, in combination with a cordon of employment and housing discrimination around inner-city neighborhoods, you saw this implosion where nothing remained for residents to do except develop illicit economies in reaction to that pullout of capital stimulus. Dr. Wilson makes the point, and I think it's applicable to Indian reservations, that you cannot fix things through self-help, because you're just socializing poverty. You have to put capital stimulus back into Indian reservations, just as you do in inner cities.

BOGHOSIAN: I wanted to ask you specifically about community members' relationship with law enforcement, because I understand you were a co-founder of the community relations council that formed a few years ago, between the city, the mayor, law enforcement, and leaders in the American Indian community. How are relationships now?

ABOUREZK: I think they've improved a little. We formed that in response to several police shootings and killings of Native Americans, and I think the law enforcement knew they were in trouble, too, and so they reached out. We used my law office as a meeting point and brought in leaders from the native community and all the law enforcement in the area. I have to give the former chief of police and the former sheriff a lot of credit. They and the mayor really worked hard with us to come up with some solutions to handling citizen complaints about the treatment of Native Americans by law enforcement.

The new chief of police I think has a great commitment to this, so hopefully we're going to see a renewed interest; but oftentimes, the power structure is not interested in doing anything until they're in crisis, and only then their minds get clear. I hope it doesn't come to that, but I do think minority communities all over are really near the boiling point, because of conditions and the reaction that we often see from law enforcement against people living there, as we saw in Ferguson.

Charles Abourezk was interviewed on Law and Disorder *on October 13, 2014, by Heidi Boghosian, Michael Ratner, and Michael Steven Smith. This interview has been edited and condensed.*

HOLLY MAGUIGAN

Holly Maguigan (b. 1945) practiced criminal defense law in Philadelphia and New York City. She taught the criminal defense clinics at CUNY Law School and at New York University School of Law. Maguigan is an expert on the criminal trials of battered women. She was on the Board of Directors of the William M. Kunstler Fund for Racial Justice and the co-president of the Society of American Law Teachers, which named her Great Teacher of 2014.

HOLLY MAGUIGAN: I started out doing medieval history at Berkeley. It was 1967 and Oakland stopped the draft. I was still interested in medieval history, but I got very interested in the anti-war politics. I'd been interested in anti-racism politics before, but I always thought I could do my main intellectual love and my political love simultaneously. They didn't have to be the same.

I hated lawyers. I really hated lawyers. They were boring, they talked about themselves all the time, they only had stories about their cases and how great they were, and they would never post bail when people got arrested. I had very little use for lawyers. But I went to a meeting, I had moved to Santa Cruz from Berkeley, and I was at a meeting planning the People's Park demonstrations in '68 in California. This guy takes the microphone and starts reading, and there's another guy in the back of the room who starts ululating. It's like right out of *Battle of Algiers*. It's unbelievable.

He came running up to the mic and grabbed the mic and said, "Every time a suit tries to read you something, stop them." He says, "There's all these surveillance cameras, they all know you're here, this means what he's reading is a John and Jane Doe injunction against the march on People's Park. They've got cameras, they can—every one of you is in criminal contempt, if you now do the march. If you let him finish reading the injunction. Now just don't ever let anybody. Just shriek, yell, do whatever sound you want to make." I thought that was so cool. That was the best. The most useful thing I'd ever seen a lawyer do in my life.

I went home. My fiancé was applying to law schools, despite my complaints. "You're much too nice a person to go to law school, you shouldn't go to law school." I was applying to history Ph.D. programs. I went home and I said, "Give me every application you haven't filled out." I took it to a copy shop and I made copies and applied to every law school whose application he hadn't finished. We were right up against the deadline.

MICHAEL RATNER: Great way to select a law school.

MAGUIGAN: It's as good as any.

MICHAEL STEVEN SMITH: Or a profession, for that matter.

MAGUIGAN: Worked out well.

We decided to go to this school that accepted us both and gave me the most money. His family had money, but mine didn't. That was the University of Pennsylvania in Philadelphia, which is where I stayed then for seventeen years.

SMITH: You had one of the pre-eminent constitutional and criminal defense law firms, Kairys, Rudovsky, and Maguigan, in Philadelphia, and you were there during a time when Frank Rizzo was the police chief and then the mayor. Let's talk about the old days in Philly. How'd you start out?

MAGUIGAN: I love that. Well, first I started out as a public defender. I loved being a public defender, it was the beginning and end of everything I had hoped it would be. It was just great.

That's where I met David Rudovsky and David Kairys. They were then defenders, when I was a student. After they went out on their own, they invited me to join them. I kept putting it off, because I loved being a defender so much.

RATNER: I've had other friends who've been public defenders. It's not an exactly wonderful job, in certain ways, because the people you meet have been so oppressed by the system, and your chances of giving them anything meaningful is very hard.

MAGUIGAN: In Philadelphia, there was much more actual litigation. Not just motion litigation, there's a lot of that here in New York City, but actual trials. Lots of trials. You really had a shot at getting somebody off. You had sense there was an analysis that people were doing life on the installment plan. That what you needed was to do what you could to kick the wood loose, any particular time.

Your clients understood that. There were limits to what you could do. The system wasn't the least bit fair, but people really appreciated the fact that there were lawyers at the Defender Association who were willing to give everything they had to get them out. It inspired you, you know what I mean? There was never a morning you got up and thought, "Why am I doing this?"

It was in many ways a difficult office to work in because, unless it was a major case, you didn't represent a client from beginning to end. For the life on the installment plan cases, the ordinary misdemeanors and low-level felonies, it was what's called vertical representation. You represented a room. Even so, you got to know people, so when you went to the jail, there were people who called your name and you knew their names. It was a community in its own odd way. It was very difficult for me to leave it. I found it very painful to leave.

SMITH: Let's fast-forward to your private practice. You're going with Kairys and Rudovsky, who I sat next to in law school because I'm Smith and he's R, and that's how it was arranged at NYU. Anyway, you all wind up in Philly. They invite you to join the firm. It was one of those famous movement firms. Talk about what the three of you did.

MAGUIGAN: We did a lot of different things. My interest was focused on criminal defense. I did police misconduct because the legal worker in that office, Jayma Abdu—a brilliant litigator who then came to New York and was office staff for the national office of the National Lawyers Guild—gave me my marching orders and told me what to do. I did what she said.

I did a lot of grand jury stuff in that time. The Patty Hearst grand jury was one of the first ones. It's where I met Bill Kunstler and Margie Ratner, now Margaret Ratner Kunstler. There was a grand jury convened. It actually met all over the country, or several of them met, to investigate the alleged transportation of Patty Hearst by the Symbionese Liberation Army [SLA] from California, where she had been captured. Kidnapped because she was a Hearst.

I got a call from the Center for Constitutional Rights about being emergency counsel, if there was a stay requested from a Harrisburg grand jury.

I was very excited, because on the phone were Bill Kunstler and Rhonda Copelon, and all these people whose names I knew, but I didn't know. They're explaining what they want me to do as if we were in the Second Circuit. It's a very New York thing. You assume the way things work in New York is the way they work everywhere, and that if everybody says that's not how they work, they think you just don't get it.

I said, "Trust me. This is Third Circuit. This is a different place. This is what they do. You file an emergency appeal, an application for a stay, they get a judge who's available. You have to go in." Apparently, they hung up the phone then and said, "We've got a live one in Philadelphia, let's rope her in." That's how I got involved.

It was fun. We went all over. We knew, ultimately, we were going to lose. You always lose. But you can cause a lot of delay and quite a bit of havoc, if you're creative and energetic.

RATNER: Were there witnesses you were representing in front of the grand jury?

MAGUIGAN: Yeah. I represented Jay Weiner, who was then a sports writer who'd been blackballed because of his connection with the sports left, remember? Jack Scott and Micki Scott, and the Mexico Olympics. The anti-racist—

RATNER: And the African Americans who raised their fist.

MAGUIGAN: Exactly.

RATNER: They were involved with those people.

MAGUIGAN: Yes. He was supposed to, after being graduated from college, go to local—I won't name it, because I'm actually kind of fond of this newspaper, but a local newspaper that then withdrew the job offer. He was working as a cook, actually not a bad cook at all, in a local vegetarian eatery in Philadelphia until the grand jury was over. He did some time. He was at Allenwood. But he got good advice from other clients of mine, so he refused to testify and was held in contempt. He wouldn't give any information at all about what he may have known about what his friends were up to.

At this point, they're looking for Patty Hearst or anybody who might've been involved in her kidnapping and transportation. This is after they had firebombed that house in Oakland. This was after a lot of tragedy. Weiner ended up going to prison, but not for all that long, because one of the things you can do is then torture the judge until he lets him out. We did that, and we got him out.

SMITH: Talk to us about Frank Rizzo and the contention between your firm and his policies.

MAGUIGAN: He was a killer. There's no question. Under his tenure as commissioner of police and then as mayor, more people died as a result of police actions than before or since. One of the amazing things was that the next mayor, who was no great shakes, saw the number of deaths decrease by 33 percent just in the first six months of his term.

It was a time when police were really green-lighted to do whatever they wanted, and told it was the right thing to do. I don't mean to suggest that all the police started out homicidal, what I mean to suggest is this was a situation in which from the top down came the message, "If you're a good cop, then you're going to take people out however you think you need to."

Rizzo himself was very sporty about it. He liked to go out in a cummerbund, in his nightclothes with the nightsticks stuck in his tuxedo cummerbund and round people up and humiliate people.

I was thinking about his invasion of the Black Panther party headquarters in Philadelphia, and his bringing out everybody who was found in there and forcing them to strip and stand naked on the street in the cold, while he walks behind them, wielding his nightstick. It was gross. It was horrible. It was really a very, very bad time.

We did a lot of criminal defense, of course. A lot of litigation against the police tactics, at all different levels. David and David did a lot of excessive force litigation. A lot of illegal search litigation. I tended to do litigation about people who were targeted more because of who they were.

The reality is, in that kind of situation, organizing is absolutely as important as litigating. It was hard sometimes to keep your eye on the ball, you know what I mean? To remind yourselves that the litigation was one piece of a strategy. That unless people made it clear that they weren't going to tolerate this police violence, a judge's ruling or a jury's decision wasn't going to matter that much.

You really have to keep being mindful of the fact that you cannot ask people to take time away from organizing for litigation. That the litigation has to be just part of the whole strategy.

RATNER: Did you develop any kind of specialty while you were working with Kairys, Rudovsky, and Maguigan?

MAGUIGAN: Kind of by accident, I did, in a way. By the time we'd worked together for several years, I thought I knew about race and class bias in the courtroom as much as a white woman who was middle-class could know.

Then, I got assigned to represent a woman who was accused of killing her abusive boyfriend. I was just blown away by what happens when you add hatred of women to hatred of black people and hatred of poor people. It stunned me. It absolutely stunned me.

I called the judge who assigned me to this homicide, to say, "Why me? Why did you assign me to this?" He said, "Oh, you just came up next." It was like, Philadelphia was very corrupt at that time, so he was one of the few judges who didn't demand money to be on the list to get—

RATNER: Unbelievable.

MAGUIGAN: I'm telling you, judges would go by in the hall and say, "Oh, Maguigan. You didn't give me anything this Christmas, not even one lousy bottle. You're not getting any assignments." Judges would do things like they'd open the drawer in their chambers, and there'd be wads of bills.

RATNER: Unbelievable.

MAGUIGAN: They'd let you know what they wanted. One time I was litigating a motion to suppress, and the judge said, "It's just about time for the lunch and recess. I bet between now and 2:15, you and your client will come up with two hundred reasons why I should rule in his favor."

RATNER: Oh my gosh. That guy's cheap.

MAGUIGAN: I know. Stunning, right? Well, it was a long time ago. If you get two hundred from everybody, you see what I mean? It's not that cheap. Two hundred is within reach for a lot of people.

RATNER: These are amazing stories.

SMITH: Michael asked you that question—

MAGUIGAN: About the specialties.

SMITH: Not to solicit your specialty in bribing judges, but your specialty in practicing law.

MAGUIGAN: I did not. Actually, I was famous for not bribing them. This guy gave me this case, because I didn't bribe anybody. He assigned me this case, for no particular reason, and I went. This was the first time to my knowledge, I now realize, I had represented a lot of women who'd been victimized by intimate partner violence. I just didn't know.

But this was the first time that I was aware that that was what was going on. What happened was, he attacked her in a restaurant, and pushed her back through the tables. She fell out of her shoes, she was knocking things off the tables as she went by, asking people for help. Crying out for people to help her, because he's strangling her and she can barely breathe.

They get to the back of the restaurant, where there's a carving table, and she picked up a knife and stabbed him in the arm, meaning to get him just in the arm. To make him stop. But because the knife was very sharp, they were in a restaurant, and because of a birth defect or a birth anomaly, his heart was very close to the wall of his chest. So the knife pierced his heart and he died instantly on the spot.

I hire an investigator. I say, "Go to this place, around the same time, and see if there are any witnesses," because it's a neighborhood place and maybe there are people who go there every evening for an early dinner. The investigator calls me and say, "You have to come here."

I went, and there were all these people in the restaurant, including a couple guys sitting at the bar. Joe turns to them and says, "Tell her what you just told me." They all look around and one guy kind of collects himself and says basically what she had said to me. He describes the scene. It starts out by the cigarette machine just inside the door. He's saying, "I'm going to kill you, I'm going to kill you," and she's asking for help and nobody's helping.

I say to him, "Why didn't you help her?" He says, "We feel so bad about it now, but at the time, we didn't know they weren't married."

I thought, "Okay, this is a whole new world."

RATNER: If they'd been married, it would've been okay.

MAGUIGAN: Right. It changed everything for me. So I developed something of a specialty in women who kill men. Although I should hastily say that some of my best friends are men.

SMITH: I appreciate that. You married one of ours, and you're actually pretty nice.

MAGUIGAN: Yes. My own personal husband is a very nice man.

RATNER: Although Michael did just—

SMITH: Pull his chair two feet farther from Holly.

RATNER: Now what year was this? Because this is the very beginning of really the establishment of this—

MAGUIGAN: Of the notion that women could claim self-defense and be reasonable. Late '70s it started. Liz Schneider was doing her work then, in New York. The Women's Self-Defense Project, the Center for Constitutional Rights, were doing their work. For me, this started in the late '70s. Then, in the early '80s, a group in Philadelphia called Women Against Abuse began working, and they did advocacy for battered women accused of crime, and it made a huge difference. It meant that we could collaborate with people who were really knowledgeable about the dynamics of intimate partner violence. We also asked them about who to use as expert witnesses, if you decided to use an expert witness, and about how to get in touch with them and what to do.

SMITH: Remarkable experience. Can you tell us now about your argument in the Supreme Court?

MAGUIGAN: There was an issue running around about a person accused of crime, and their right to cross-examine certain statements. It was a question about the Sixth Amendment and the right to do it. It was coming up in the Ninth Circuit, which is California, and in the Third Circuit, which is mainly Pennsylvania, although also Delaware and parts of New Jersey.

We were aware of all the litigation that was going on, and I was trying a case with this guy who was characterized by the newspapers as a rogue ex-cop, who taught me a lot, actually. He taught me how to move, because he used to arrest what then we called second-story men. He taught me about how you get a double Hefty garbage bag, and you tie it with a square knot, and you can carry almost anything. Since then, I've never moved any other way. I only move with garbage bags. They're very strong, they're very forgiving.

I'd represented him for years. He got in all kinds of entertaining trouble, and it was fun. Mainly we won, and David Rudovsky and I collaborated on a couple cases. Sometimes they went after him and they would search his house and then David would sue them for the Fourth Amendment violation and earn enough money to pay our fee and that just annoyed them so much.

This case we lost. We appealed it to the Third Circuit, but appealed it having made a record that we knew satisfied the standards of the Ninth Circuit and the Third Circuit. Arguably, that was a tactical error, because then, when the government applied for cert—a "petition for certiorari" is an application to the Supreme Court to hear an appeal, which they wouldn't hear as of right in most criminal appeals. You have to petition for certiorari in order to get the Supremes to hear it.

They petitioned, and I say to my friends, "We are dead in the water. This is it, they're going to grant cert in our case, and not one of the Ninth Circuit cases, and we are so dead." By this time, David and David had stopped doing quite so much litigation. Dave Rudovsky had been the trainer for the Defender Association, and David Kairys was moving into teaching, so I had started this other firm with Edmund Tiryak and Julie Shapiro and Leslie Engel to do more litigation.

By the time this case went to the Supreme Court, that was the team. Once the cert petition was granted, which meant the Supreme Court was going to hear the appeal, it was over. It was totally over. I said to them, "We cannot let this take over our lives. It's true, it's the major leagues. On the other hand, we could write the best brief in history, or submit no brief at all, and we're going to have [Thurgood] Marshall and [William] Brennan dissenting. We could do the best argument ever, or fall down in a dead faint from panic, and we'll have Marshall and Brennan—let's not forget, this is six troglodytes and three dweebs, and it's just not going to work out for us. Our team is not going to win here."

We tried really hard not to get caught up in it, but there is a mystique about arguing in the Supreme Court. We ended up putting a whole lot of energy into the brief, and a whole lot of energy into the argument. In the end, do I need to say, we had Marshall and Brennan dissenting? There was no choice.

Anyway, it was entertaining. It was fun. It was kind of exciting. My mother came. Oh, actually, this particular charge was a charge of manufacturing methamphetamine. I practiced. I wanted to say to the Justices, "Excuse me,

Mr. Chief Justice. Justices. Could we not mention methamphetamine? My mother's here. She thinks I'm a civil rights lawyer."

SMITH: You see why Holly's a great trial lawyer. She's one of the best storytellers we've ever had on the show. You can just see it. You can see me being on the jury. I just want to hear more from her, right? How did you get from doing this kind of mischief in Philadelphia to teaching in New York?

MAGUIGAN: There were several reasons. One was the battered women's cases I was working on were quite consuming, because people then didn't know very much about how to try these cases. The judges expected you to plead insanity, or just to plead guilty. Reasonable doubt was a consideration at sentencing, not at trial, know what I mean?

There were cases that really did require teams. I found that I was spending a lot of time working with trial teams on other cases, trying to help them get up to speed with Women Against Abuse, which is a group that turned into the National Clearing House for the Defense of Battered Women. The only national group that provides backup for these cases.

Part of it was wanting to have a situation where I could do that work without exhausting myself and all our resources, because you don't get paid to do that kind of stuff. We did need to make a little bit of money. We never made very much money. Most of the best criminal defense lawyers I know never made very much money. But you do need some. You need to pay for the repairs on the copy machine, and you need to pay your rent.

Anyway, that was one reason. Another was that my daughter, who was then six, would get up in the morning on weekends and come into my bedroom and wake me up and say, "Are witnesses coming over today?" I hadn't started out as a single parent, but once I became a single parent, I felt guilty all the time. Either I was at the prisons and jails and meeting with my clients, or doing investigation and meeting with witnesses, or I was taking care of my daughter. Whichever I was doing, I felt dreadful.

SMITH: Your daughter's name is Miranda, and I wanted to sidetrack here about why . . . We're not talking about Shakespeare and *The Tempest*, are we?

MAGUIGAN: No, we're not, no. Actually, when I was pregnant, I used to go around City Hall and Philadelphia. I answered, "Ready." On every case. Do you have any idea how fun it is to try a case when you're hugely pregnant? Oh, it was the best. Talk about the juries wanting to hear me, they couldn't take their eyes off you. All you had to do was move a shoulder, and they would go—they were sure you were going into labor. No chance that any terrible witness would be listened to, you know what I mean? Somebody gets up and says something bad about your client, and you are just moving around in your chair a little bit. Nobody can listen to him.

All right. I'd walk around answering, "Ready," on every case, and people'd say, "What are you going to name the baby?" I'd say, "Miranda. After *Miranda v. Arizona.*" It's the case where the Supreme Court held that the Fifth Amendment due process clause secures your Sixth Amendment right to counsel. The police have to tell you that you have a right to a lawyer before they interrogate you, if you're in custody.

SMITH: You know, there's another *Miranda* right, with reference to Carmen Miranda, the exotic dancer. You have a right to wear fruit on your head and dance funny.

MAGUIGAN: As Miranda did many, many Halloweens. I'd say, "Miranda, unless it's a boy, in which case Gideon." Which was the original right to counsel case. A friend of mine took me aside, Linda Backiel actually, who's in the Lawyers Guild now in Puerto Rico, took me out to dinner and said, "You know, you're wrong to make jokes about the name Miranda, because outside of a small circle of perverts, more people will think of *The Tempest* than will think of the Fifth Amendment rights of an accused rapist."

I go home and I say that to her father, and Paul says, "Your friends are so weird." First of all, it's your small circle of perverts. Second of all, the character in *The Tempest* is the most male-identified female you can imagine, right? She gets handed off from her father, to a sprite, to a boyfriend. I mean, please. Miranda was sort of a joke, but off the table.

Then she was born, and she seemed like a Miranda. Before we left the hospital, we debated back and forth, and finally he came in and he said, "I did it." I said, "What did you do?" "She's Miranda MAGUIGAN-Tully. That's it. We can call her something else, we can change it within ninety days, we can—"

Not long after that, I get a call from our friend, who says, "Richie's really in trouble this time. You have to go and represent him at the hearing." I said, "I don't have to go. I've got a baby who's like a week old. I'm on maternity leave, I definitely don't have to go." She says, "Just go buy the newspapers and look who's on the front page."

I went and I looked and I go, "Okay, Richie's really in trouble this time."

He was a friend of a friend, who'd been in trouble several times and this was really a serious one. I go to the courthouse, and as I'm walking to the courthouse, I run into a detective, who says, "We arrested Gene So-and-so last night." I said, "I know, you let him call me. Thanks a lot, you let him call me at three in the morning. I'm a nursing mother, what was that?"

He goes, "We arrested him. Like we always do." It's true, they always did arrest him. "We say to him, like we always do, 'So Gene. What are you going to do for yourself?' He wouldn't give us anything." I say, "I know, you let him—" The way it worked was, if he wasn't going to talk, they'd let him call me, but if he already talked then he wouldn't call me. It was not like calling me was significant except to wake me up in the middle of the night.

He says, "No, no, no. Are you going to listen or you going to talk?" I say, "Okay, I'll listen." "So we arrested Gene the way we always do. We take him into the district, the way we always do. We say to him, like we always do, 'Gene, what are you going to do for yourself?'" And he says, "'What am I going to do for myself? What am I going to do for myself? Do you know who my lawyer is? Do you know what she named her baby?'"

It was fabulous. It was seen as an act of total solidarity by my clients. Every facility I went into after she was born had pictures of her up with little bars in front.

We move to New York. First to CUNY, and I have to say, I'm so grateful to CUNY Law School for giving me that chance. I was a totally untried teacher. I had taught trial advocacy as an adjunct, but I had never been a full-time teacher. They took me on and it was great. The students were great and my colleagues were great and I realized, this is what I want to do.

But, I missed court. In those years, this was 1986, '87, and CUNY didn't yet have a criminal defense clinic. So, I moved to NYU. I didn't need to be trying the cases, but I wanted to be in court. I wanted to be in the presence of that conflict between the authorities and regular people and see what could be done.

I went to NYU, where I taught in the criminal defense clinic for many years. Had a wonderful time. To see students react to the great stories that their clients have is just amazing, because it's all about loving people, right? It's all about being fascinated by the stories. People accused of crime get into such wonderful pickles, and it's just—

Miranda likes to tell a story about a client who's—New York, the prosecutors are required, at arraignment, the first appearance before a judge, to give you what's called statement notice. They have to tell you what statements they intend to use against your client at trial. They have a certain number of days to do it, usually they do it at the arraignment.

One client's statement notice was, "What can I say? I was in the wrong place, at the wrong time, doing the wrong thing." It's Miranda's favorite. When I told her that story, it was like, "Okay, that's it. Nobody's ever going to get better than that. That was the best."

SMITH: Let's talk about your experience practicing law, and what you brought into the classroom. I can tell you that having a teacher like you would've been a great thing for me. Most of my teachers never knew how to practice law, they were just good law students.

MAGUIGAN: I think it's true. A lot of teachers in law school, who are terrific at theory, haven't ever practiced. They don't accept that they're teaching in a trade school. You're teaching somebody how to do something that matters hugely. But it's not necessarily a Ph.D. program, and a lot of people really think of it in that way, a lot of people who have the job of teaching at law schools.

Now, CUNY doesn't do that. CUNY professors are people who've practiced. A lot of people at NYU have practiced. But you're right that the students really appreciate the fact that you've practiced, because you can talk about how things work and don't work. You can talk about how fact-specific the implementation of every legal principle is. If facts are slightly different, then the outcome is going to be affected, even though the principle stays the same.

And at a clinic, practice is key. It's hard to imagine how you could teach a clinic and supervise student practice if you hadn't yourself gone through the highs and the lows. It was interesting teaching students how to cope with panic, because I don't know a criminal defense lawyer who hasn't panicked. You always panicked.

It strikes me, actually, that you cannot do the job if you don't go from, "Anybody could win this case, your parrot Charlie could win this case, anybody could win this case," to then thinking, "This case cannot be won. Certainly not by me. I am in the Slough of Despond now, there's no way this case is going to be won." And then to climbing out of that valley of fear and thinking, "Okay, there's pieces of work to do, we can do it."

I think it's useful for students to have somebody who doesn't think that the panic is bad, who sees the panic as something that motivates you, who understands that it's a human response to having responsibility for another person. It makes total sense to me. It seems to me if you don't have it, you're not feeling everything you ought to be feeling.

RATNER: That's a remarkably good statement, Holly, I really appreciate it.

SMITH: You got active in the Society of American Law Teachers (SALT), and I want to talk about that because it's a wonderful organization. I only wish that there was a SALT around when we were in law schools, but there's one now. Talk to us about what SALT does.

MAGUIGAN: When I started teaching, not so much when I was at CUNY but once I got to NYU, I started going to conferences. It took me a year to just get my feet under me for teaching, and it took me a while to realize that there were conferences where I could learn things.

I was used to the National Lawyers Guild, and the National Conference of Black Lawyers, and La Raza, and the Women in Law Conference. I kept going to these conferences and thinking, "Where are the regular people? There's no regular people here." The people who swear, and who get tired, and cranky, and every so often hate their students, you know what I mean? The regular people. The students seemed kind of irrelevant in a lot of these conferences. It was about scholarship, and teaching at a certain level.

Then I went to my first SALT conference. It was all regular people. That's what SALT is about. Hazel Weiser, who's a stalwart of SALT and a former executive director, sums it up this way: "SALT is about who gets into law school, what they learn, and who teaches them." It's about access to justice, and it's about relating to law school as a place where you train people to do social justice, or to enable social justice, or to work with people who are going to make social justice happen.

SALT's focus is on students and teaching. It's not that SALT members don't care about scholarship, because scholarship can often make a huge difference. But the teaching part is key to them. That's so refreshing. It was probably in 1988 or '89 that I went to my first SALT conference, and I never looked back. I've been going to SALT teaching conferences ever since, and I've been a member of the Board of Directors of SALT, and I'm a past co-president of SALT. SALT has meant a huge amount in my life, since I've been a teacher. It's actually been a defining institution for me.

RATNER: What you would recommend to people about becoming lawyers?

MAGUIGAN: I think you have to love gossip, and love stories. And love hearing stories and love hearing them more than once. And figuring out how to tell that story, how to enable the person to tell her or his own story, when he or she is able. Not everybody accused of crime is able to withstand the stress and actually tell it. But that's the main thing.

But then you need to love codes. A lot of people who like law like crossword puzzles, because they like filling in the blanks. A lot of people, as it turns out, who like law like medieval history, because a lot of it is about parsing little bits of information to try to see what the whole story is, and tease it out.

But I think it's really, more than anything, it's about liking people and wanting to see what you can do to help them extricate themselves from a problem.

Holly Maguigan was interviewed on Law and Disorder *on August 17, 2015, by Michael Ratner and Michael Steven Smith. This interview has been edited and condensed.*

JAN SUSLER

Jan Susler (b. 1949) joined the People's Law Office in Chicago in 1982. She litigates and advocates on behalf of prisoners and represents people wrongfully imprisoned, falsely arrested and subjected to excessive force and abuse. She has worked on behalf of the Puerto Rican independence movement, successfully representing nationalist Oscar López Rivera, a longtime political prisoner, securing his release in 2017. Susler is a leader of the National Lawyers Guild and is part of its National Police Accountability Project.

HEIDI BOGHOSIAN: When you went to law school, did you have an idea that you would become what we call a people's lawyer?

JAN SUSLER: It's why I went to law school. It was a dream.

MICHAEL STEVEN SMITH: I imagine you didn't find it a really great experience.

SUSLER: Oh, God . . .

SMITH: I wanted to ask you, what did you do when you finally escaped?

SUSLER: Well, I escaped through the process, I did wait until it was done. I mean, the National Lawyers Guild was just an amazing . . . I don't want to call it a refuge, but when I went to law school, women were 10 percent of the class and really resented. I mean, I remember the class before us had to walk out just to get a pot to piss in; they really had to stage a walk out to get a bathroom. It was a hostile environment. Lots of rich white boys who thought they were all that, but the Guild and actually, the GI Bill evened things out class-wise, which was a delight. I worked at legal aid and while I was in law school, it kept me sane along with the Guild. My first job was at a law school clinic, which was a little ironic since I didn't know what the hell I was doing, but I was supposed to teach law students.

It was called prison legal aid. It was at Southern Illinois University and we provided civil, legal services to state prisoners, which is a wonderful experience and also a big eye-opener, both for me and my students. The majority of the people we were serving were African American and Latino men from Chicago who were in a very hostile, southern Illinois, redneck environment and being watched over by mostly white guards. It was very eye-opening to see what was being done in my name and in the public's name, but the public didn't really know about it.

Through that process of doing abortion rights work, anti-death-penalty work, and prisoners' rights work through the Guild, I met the folks at the People's Law Office.

BOGHOSIAN: How did you get involved with the Puerto Rican independence movement?

SUSLER: At around the same time as I was working on prison legal aid, my law partner called me up and said, "There's a couple of Puerto Rican radicals who've been sent to the state prison near where you are doing your work and you need to go see them because they're quite at risk. The state considers them to be enemies and they're very far from their home and their community and you have got to go see them." I did. That was one of those trite cliché things, "and the rest is history," but it's true. I met two of the then eleven Puerto Rican political prisoners, who opened my eyes to something I knew nothing about. I knew nothing about Puerto Rico being a U.S. colony, having been invaded, them resisting colonialism, I learned about international law, making colonialism a crime against humanity, and then I started traveling to the Puerto Rican community in Chicago and then to Puerto Rico. They really opened my world and what a gift they gave me, what a privilege it's been for me.

In the late '70s, the Guild created a Puerto Rico legal project to go to Puerto Rico and work with Puerto Rican lawyers and activists in the independence movement and people who were trying to get the U.S. Navy out of the small Puerto Rican island of Vieques. There was, in the U.S., a Puerto Rican solidarity movement but, through the Guild, we were able to breathe new life into that and create a Puerto Rico subcommittee and try to keep Puerto Rico on the radar screen. Central America was more sexy, I think, for the left, in the Guild, than Puerto Rico, so it's been a bit of a struggle.

SMITH: Jan, talk to us about your Puerto Rican *independentista* clients. How did you first meet them, what they did they do, and what have you been able to do for them?

SUSLER: Very few people ever get to meet people who are so committed to freedom and the freedom of their people, and it makes them very special that they were willing to risk life and limb and basically give up their children, their families, their careers for the freedom of their country. I think people in the U.S. understand who Nelson Mandela is and what he stood for and what he sacrificed, and what he meant for his country. These men and women are the same for the people of Puerto Rico.

For me, it's been quite a privilege. They were artists and working in universities. Most had college degrees but really understood that colonialism was a crime against humanity, and they organized clandestinely, into an organization called The Armed Forces for National Liberation. They were arrested in the early 1980s and accused of seditious conspiracy, which at the time was a statute that had only been used against people in the Puerto Rican independence movement. Very selective prosecution basically, because the government didn't really have to prove anything except that they agreed to be part of this organization. Didn't have to prove that they did anything. It's a tool in the government's arsenal, to try to really stop the independence movement in its tracks.

SMITH: Len Weinglass used to call it the "darling law" for prosecutors.

SUSLER: They got astronomical sentences, even though they hadn't hurt or killed anyone, and they got put away, some of them in the most maximum-security prisons in the U.S., in the control unit. My job was to advocate for their human rights and to educate about their situation. They refuse to accept the jurisdiction of the U.S. court, so we had a challenge to try to figure out how to do this without resorting to the court, which is sometimes the first thing lawyers think about.

BOGHOSIAN: In 1999, the president commuted some of their sentences.

SUSLER: Very true. It was a historic movement. I don't think that in the history of the U.S., that anything like that's ever happened before—and many people say, "Oh, how did you do that? You're so wonderful!" I have one role to play; many thousands of other people had other roles to play in convincing the president of the United States that that was convenient for him to do in terms of how the international community and the human rights community in Puerto Rico and the U.S. would appreciate that as a gesture of good faith.

BOGHOSIAN: What do you think of the current political climate in this country? You are hoping President Obama will also commute sentences. But with the crack down on so-called domestic terrorists in Puerto Rico, how do you see the political environment now versus thirty years ago?

SUSLER: The world has changed. The stakes are different. What was then called terrorism, that doesn't compare to what's going on today. The intervention of the United States in the political activities and in the daily lives of people in the U.S. and all over the world is at a level that's unprecedented. It's a very, very different political environment. President Obama, unfortunately, has accumulated the worst record in the history of U.S. presidents for commutations and pardons, and I think he was, in part, influenced by the atmosphere of hysteria and fear that the right has been able to generate.

I think it's never been easy for the people in the Puerto Rican independence movement. We're not looking for it to be easy here, but we are continuing to organize. We're not going to stop until we get everybody out of prison and until we get Puerto Rico independent.

BOGHOSIAN: Have you been involved at all in the police torture cases in Chicago?

SUSLER: Certainly in terms of being part of the People's Law Office. My work hasn't really focused on the torture cases here. We do a variety of police misconduct, civil rights litigation. There have been wrongful convictions I've been involved with where there've been false confessions coerced and fabricated. Your average, routine police misconduct, beating, shooting, killing, jail suicides, all that sort of thing, are done in our names. One of my sisters said to me, "How can you do it? You see just so many horrible, negative things. How do you do it every day and for all these years?" I say, "Well, one of the things you don't realize is that when you meet people who have been through experiences like that, it's very therapeutic for them to fight back to expose what was done to them." The fight to get justice for them is very life-giving and really, a wonderful thing to be able to do with your professional life. To work with people who really are not going to just sit back and take it. I don't look at it as having to deal with the horrible, negative things. I look at it as helping people understand what is being done in their name, by their law enforcement and their city administration or their state administration, and resisting and fighting back.

Jan Susler was interviewed on Law and Disorder *on September 30, 2013, by Heidi Boghosian and Michael Steven Smith. This interview has been edited and condensed.*

BILL GOODMAN

William H. (Bill) Goodman is a partner in the Detroit civil rights law firm Goodman and Hurwitz. He is a former president of the National Lawyers Guild, a former legal director of the Center for Constitutional Rights, and currently on the Board of Directors of the Sugar Law Center. Bill Goodman is the son of Ernie Goodman, the great lawyer and former president of the National Lawyers Guild.

HEIDI BOGHOSIAN: *The Color of Law: Ernie Goodman, Detroit, and the Struggle for Labor and Civil Rights* is the title of a recent book recreating the compelling story of Ernie Goodman, one of the nation's preeminent defense attorneys for workers and the militant poor. Authors Steve Babson, Dave Riddle, and David Elsila tell the story from Goodman's early years as a corporate lawyer to his conversion to labor law during the Great Depression. From Detroit to Mississippi, Goodman saw police and other officials giving the "color of law" to actions that stifled freedom of speech and nullified the rights of workers and minorities.

This book demonstrates that the abuse of power is non-partisan and that individuals who oppose injustice can change the course of events. To talk more about the book, we're joined by Ernie Goodman's son, and an extraordinary public interest lawyer in his own right, Bill.

Bill, what's your reaction to the book?

BILL GOODMAN: I think the book is really surprisingly delightful because it goes beyond my dad as just an individual person who led a wonderful life, to talk as well about the experience of the '20s through into the '70s, and what it meant to be an engaged and involved person in the politics of that period.

MICHAEL RATNER: I think so as well, Bill. I read it and I just thought it really brought alive your dad and the period he was in. Why don't you talk to us a little bit about what you consider some of the most significant parts of your dad's legal and political life.

GOODMAN: Well, without a doubt, and I think the book makes this point so vividly, his wakening as a political person came about during the emergence and early days of the UAW [United Automobile Workers]: the sit-down strike in Flint, the beginnings of the labor movement just before that, and then organizing the contract with the Ford Motor Company. That was really an incredibly important period for him and for the country and his role was instrumental. He was one of the key people who provided legal representation and counseling and tactics strategy to the UAW, which was the most progressive labor union in the United States at that time.

RATNER: We always hear about the Flint sit-downs but you know, probably a lot of our listeners may not be aware of what they were and how recently—really—they occurred.

GOODMAN: The UAW tried to stage a few experimental sit-downs before the Flint sit-downs. It's discussed in the book. The sit-downs in Flint themselves were in 1937. The workers literally took over the factories from General Motors, the most powerful corporation in the United States at the time. The question was whether the governor was going to send in the troops and basically kick the workers out and probably hurt or, perhaps, kill some of them.

Governor Frank Murphy, a progressive figure in Michigan politics in many ways, refused to send in the troops. This was a key moment. The UAW and the labor movement have been instrumental in the election of Frank Murphy for the governorship. That was it. But taking over, literally taking power and grabbing these factories away from these huge corporations, that was enormously important. Symbolic.

RATNER: At some point, your father and the firm he was with stopped representing, really, the UAW. What happened?

GOODMAN: He worked for a man named Maurice Sugar, who was a very important figure in American politics and the law at that time. Both of them were founding members of the National Lawyers Guild. Sugar was fired as the general counsel for the UAW because of the beginnings of the Cold War. Walter Reuther, who was an interesting figure and dynamic figure in American labor history, decided that he was going to ride the wave of the Cold War and anti-Communism and, basically, get rid of the radicals and Communists within the union.

So they fired Sugar and my dad along with him. As a result, they could no longer represent most labor unions, although they continued to represent a few progressive ones and progressive UAW locals. They then were stuck with representing all of those people who were being attacked in the McCarthy period in front of the House Un-American Activities Committee, in the Smith Act trials in which communism was put on trial as an idea and as a system of thought. The First Amendment was not a protection.

These were the early days of their representation and this firm, the first non-segregated, interracial law firm in the United States, started out with its black partner, George Crockett, who later became a congressman in prison, for contempt in the Foley Square Smith Act trial.

RATNER: That's one of my favorite stories. I know you knew George Crockett really well. And I knew him, not as well as you, but pretty well. He was an amazing figure and, of course, he was your dad's partner. As you said, it was the first, we think, interracial law firm in the United States and it's quite extraordinary. I know you were a member of that firm as well.

GOODMAN: I was, and Crockett was one of the most courageous people that I've ever known in my life in many ways. He would not bend and he was continually attacked for asserting and protecting the Constitution of the United States and I just have huge admiration for the man.

BOGHOSIAN: Bill, the book also talks about your father's involvement with the Attica defense. Can you talk about that a bit?

GOODMAN: I can talk about Attica. Actually, he got involved in the Attica case because of me. At that time, I decided to start organizing lawyers from Detroit to start going to Buffalo and representing defendants who were charged in the Attica uprising. As we all know, at the Attica prison, there was an uprising between September ninth and September thirteenth of 1971, at which time, Nelson Rockefeller sent in state troopers and the National Guard. More than three-dozen people were killed, all by gunshots. The prisoners had no guns. No hostages were killed except by gunshot, which means they were shot by the state troopers.

As a result of that, there was a grand jury and there were criminal prosecutions against leaders of the prisoners, who were leaders of the uprising. My dad had got one of those cases. He decided he wanted to take one. Well, he took the case for Shango Bahati Kakawana, also known as Bernard Stroble, who was from Detroit and really wanted my dad to represent him. That was one of the first major trials and the first one that we won. We showed to a jury that the prosecution hid information from the jury, and hid information from the defense. They tried to cover up that they had murdered people at Attica and put the blame on people who were not to blame, the ways in which they had used snitches and informants, and had threatened and coerced people.

This was all put on trial. We won in this case, and I was honored to be part of that trial team along with my dad and along with Shango, who was *pro se* on one of the counts, and along with the wonderful, unforgettable Haywood Burns.

MICHAEL STEVEN SMITH: Bill, let's talk about your father and the Civil Rights Federation and your father's involvement very early in the civil rights movement. Your father is a movement lawyer. He was out there as the head of the Civil Rights Federation in Detroit back in the '30s. I wanted to ask you about that, and then bring it forward to your father's work as president of the

National Lawyers Guild, and his working in Mississippi during the civil rights movement twenty years later.

GOODMAN: The Civil Rights Congress had been formed in 1946, when we were still in the throes of reaction to the Reconstruction period following the Civil War: the growth of the Klan, the tax assault on African Americans at that time, an increase in murders, violence, lynchings of all sorts. My dad became very involved in this and was one of the active people in the Civil Rights Congress at that time, and the Civil Rights Federation, which was its earlier title.

This movement brought a number of very progressive African American people into progressive politics: people like Coleman Young, for example, who was very involved during that period; Crockett was another. This work was formative for my father in understanding the importance of race and racism as well as in his ideas about how to build a law firm, how to represent people, and how he became an important representative of many of the most oppressed people in the city of Detroit at that time, which was the African American community largely.

Then, of course, we know that after the pall of McCarthyism lessened in the late '50s, the civil rights movement, the most vital movement in the country and maybe in the century, took hold: the Freedom Rides in 1961; the development of Freedom Summer.

My dad and Crockett and our law firm, primarily, took the lead within the National Lawyers Guild of saying, "This has to be the priority of the Guild to represent the civil rights movement; to be the lawyers for this movement."

They started a law office in Jackson, Mississippi, in the summer of '64. Crockett was the head of it and another African American lawyer from our firm, Judge Claudia Morcum, ran the office for about approximately a year in 1965. It did major, formative things and was a center of the civil rights movement during that period.

RATNER: Your dad, one of the key people along with Crockett in the Southern civil rights movement, saw that early on there was an issue about the left credentials of the Guild and other groups—I think the NAACP LDF [National Association for Colored People Legal Defense and Education Fund]—wanting to push the Guild out of the South.

GOODMAN: There was some of that and there was an attempt, and it was also part of COINTELPRO. The FBI was behind a good deal of this; to say to the rest of the civil rights movement, to Martin Luther King, certainly, the Southern Christian Leadership Conference, and other rubes of the NAACP as well, that you're now getting in bed with Communists, and you better be careful and draw back and not involve yourself with the Guild. This became, in many ways, a negative factor, but in some ways, it forced the rest of the American legal profession to form a number of other grass roots law offices, such as the Lawyers' Committee for Civil Rights, that went down to Mississippi and Alabama as well.

There was a proliferation of civil rights law firms and they all ended up working closely together, but there certainly was an attempt to split the civil rights movement around the left credentials of the Guild.

BOGHOSIAN: Bill, as one of the most respected constitutional lawyers in this country, was there ever a doubt that you would follow in your father's footsteps?

GOODMAN: Did I ever doubt it or did he ever doubt it? It flowed pretty naturally, from my experience. I went to law school almost as a second choice because my grades weren't quite good enough to get me into graduate school and start in a career of teaching. So I decided to go to law school, and I'm very happy about that decision.

I went to law school in Chicago. I think I was the first student member of the National Lawyers Guild in many years. I was sworn in as a member to help organize the Chicago chapter of the Guild. The following summer, after my first year in law school, I went down south and worked for a civil rights law firm, Jordon, Dolly, and Holt, and specifically for Len Holt, who is one of the heroes of the civil rights movement. That was a very formative experience for me.

After that, there was no way that I was going to turn back on what I saw as the only way to conscientiously follow the law and enforce the Constitution.

SMITH: Talk about your dad starting off as a corporate lawyer, came from a poor emigrant family in rural Michigan, moved to Detroit and was hoping to make a living. Then the Depression hits and he gets politicized. What lessons do we have from the arc of your father's career?

GOODMAN: I don't know what lessons. People can draw their own lessons from other people in their own lives. What happened with him was that he was born in rural Michigan. They moved into the Jewish ghetto in Detroit. When he was five years old, he started school and then tried to be successful as a first-generation child of Jewish immigrants. I wouldn't call him a corporate lawyer, but he tried to represent small business accounts whenever he could and collect debts. He became a collection lawyer and then saw this whole society suddenly, with the crash of the stock market in 1929, crumble around him and saw people in huge, enormous need. Not so different than what we see walking around the streets of Detroit today, by the way.

He asked himself if there must be a better way to do this and saw the possibilities through the beginning of the labor movement at that time and his beginnings of understanding, at least, the principles of Socialism, which called on society to exert through its government some social conscience. He saw another approach and I think that's, as you say, the arc of what he perceived at that point.

Bill Goodman was interviewed on Law and Disorder *on November 1, 2010, by Heidi Boghosian, Michael Ratner, and Michael Steven Smith. This interview has been edited and condensed.*

CRIMINALIZING THE COMMUNIST PARTY

The Alien and Registration Act ("Smith Act") of 1940 was proposed by Congressman Howard Smith of Virginia, a poll tax supporter and a leader of the anti-labor bloc in Congress. Signed into law by President Franklin Roosevelt, it was the first statute since the Alien and Sedition Acts of 1798 to make mere advocacy of ideas a federal crime.

Federal Bureau of Investigation director J. Edgar Hoover, immensely proud of his leading role in the government's nationwide persecution and deportation of radicals and immigrants during the 1919 Palmer Raids, suggested to President Harry Truman in 1948 that the Smith Act be used against the Communist Party and its sympathizers. Truman embraced the idea as a means to outflank Republican rivals who were accusing the Democrats of being "soft" on Communism. Going after domestic Communists also complemented his international policy of subduing "subversion" in Greece, Italy, and France, where Communism was widely popular and Communist parties could conceivably take shared or total control of the national government. The most significant political heresy trial in U.S. history would bring the Cold War home.

The eleven defendants were not charged with any overt acts. The accusation was that "they conspired . . . to organize as the Communist Party and willfully to advocate and teach the principles of Marxist-Leninism," which the government alleged to mean "overthrowing and destroying the government of the United States by force and violence" at some unspecified future time. They were also accused of conspiring to "publish and circulate . . . books, articles, magazines, and newspapers advocating the principles of Marxism-Leninism," again as interpreted by the prosecution. *The Communist Manifesto* by Marx and Engels, Lenin's *State and Revolution*, and Stalin's *Foundation of Leninism* were placed into evidence as books from which the defendants taught. Among the eleven charged were Gil Green, a long-time Party leader; Eugene Dennis and Henry Winston, leaders of the national organization; John Gates, editor of the *Daily Worker*; and Gus Hall, leader of the party in Ohio. The nine-month trial took place in New York City. Some four hundred police were detailed to the Foley Square courthouse, further feeding an aura of tension and potential violence.

Judge Harold Medina suffused both the pretrial and trial proceedings with consistent prejudicial rulings and quips that were often anti-Communist or racist in nature. At one point, Medina called black defendant Benjamin J. Davis, a Harvard graduate from a distinguished Southern family, "boy." The jury was selected in a manner that ensured all of its members were at least upper-middle class. One showed overt prejudice before the trial even started, but was not dismissed.

The defendants fought the thought-crime nature of the proceedings and the government's caricaturing of their views. They claimed, to no avail, that they were for majority rule and against violence, except as a means of self-defense. Given the climate of hysteria generated by the mass media, guilty verdicts for all were more or less foreordained. Ten got and served five years in federal prison and had to pay fines of $10,000. The eleventh defendant, Robert G. Thompson, a bearer of the World War II Distinguished Service Cross for bravery, received his government's gratitude in the form of a slightly shorter sentence of only three years. Four of the defendants forfeited their bail during the appeal process and went underground where they functioned for years before surrendering or being apprehended. While in prison, Robert G. Thompson had his skull crushed by a group of Yugoslav fascists armed with a pipe, and Winston, denied essential medical care, was left blinded. Each of the defense attorneys was cited for contempt and served a prison sentence. Among those who served six months was George C. Crockett, an African American attorney who, later in his career, was first elected as a judge in Detroit's criminal court and then as a Michigan congressman.

The Truman administration's use of the Smith Act against the top leadership of the Communist Party drove a large stake into the heart not only of the party but of every organization in which the Communists had been active and influential. Not least of the indirect casualties was the newly formed Progressive Party. The indictments in the case came on the very eve of the Progressive Party's convention and appeared timed to undermine support for the new party. The Communist Party, which was heavily involved in the Progressive movement, had expected the new party to garner between four and eight million votes. The indictments and the charge that the Progressive Party was just a front for Communism were major factors in its ultimately receiving closer to one million.

The convicted Communists appealed their cases, but in 1951 the Supreme Court upheld the convictions by a vote of six (including four Truman appointees) to two. Chief Justice Fred Vinson wrote the decision for the majority. Justices Hugo Black and William O. Douglas dissented. Black noted that the government indictment was "a virulent form of prior censorship of speech and press" which is forbidden by the First Amendment and therefore unconstitutional.

Douglas wrote of his belief that the Communist Party was impotent and that "only those held by fear and panic could think otherwise." Therefore, the party could not possibly represent a "clear and present danger" as required in the law. Douglas made clear the distinction between defending the party's legal rights and supporting its positions. He pointed to the party's uncritical support of the government of the Soviet Union and quoted Andrei Vishinsky, the chief prosecutor at the third Moscow purge trial, who had written, "In our state, naturally there could be no place for freedom of speech, press, and so on for the foes of Socialism."

An ironic aspect of the convictions, which was not lost among civil libertarians and others, was that the Communist Party had fully supported the use in 1941 of the Smith Act against the leaders of the Socialist Workers Party.

Motivated by its hatred of Trotskyist political opponents and its fervent support for the Soviet-American alliance of World War II, the party had judged the Smith Act perfectly constitutional and the subsequent trials a legitimate government action. Those positions gravely undercut the credibility of the party's efforts in the 1950s to characterize the Smith Act as unconstitutional and to mobilize a defense on the basis of political free speech and freedom of association.

The criminal convictions of the leadership of the Communist Party deprived it of legitimacy in the eyes of most Americans. Although membership in the party did not significantly decline, the party was unable to recruit many new members. More significant was the damage to Party fronts and peripheral organizations. Participation of former sympathizers fell away dramatically. Long-established groups became inactive or dissolved, and the creation of new groups virtually ceased. Among the allied groups whose demise was most damaging was the International Workers Order (IWO), an insurance and fraternal order with approximately 150,000 members. Although financially sound and not directly connected to the Communist Party, the IWO was forced to dissolve in 1954 on the basis that it was a subversive organization. In addition to the political loss this entailed for the party, it also deprived Communists of an institution from which they could borrow to finance their legal defense.

After the Smith Act convictions, Hoover, disappointed that only eleven Communists had been prosecuted, wrote Truman criticizing him as "insincere" for not indicting greater numbers. This failing was soon corrected. In 1951, twenty-three more leaders were indicted, including the legendary Elizabeth Gurley Flynn, who had first burst onto the American political scene as an organizer and orator for the IWW. Flynn, a founding member of the American Civil Liberties Union, had squared off with Hoover in the 1920s when she fought for the victims of the Palmer Raids and the 101 members of the Industrial Workers of the World who were sentenced to prison at a mass trial in Chicago. In 1953, Flynn and her codefendants were fined and imprisoned.

Further indictments followed throughout the nation. In the end, over 140 Communist Party leaders were indicted. The trials did not cease until a number of Supreme Court decisions in 1957. Two of the most important were *Yates v. United States* and *Watkins v. United States*. The *Yates* decision overthrew the convictions of the second tier of Communist leaders. It drew a sharp distinction between the advocacy of an idea for purposes of incitement and the teaching of an idea as an abstract concept. In *Watkins* the Court ruled that a defendant who had opted not to use the Fifth Amendment could still use the First Amendment against "abuses of the legislative process." The vote was six to one, with Chief Justice Earl Warren writing the majority opinion.

The net effect of these and related decisions was to bring prosecutions to a halt. The Court had reaffirmed constitutional protections regarding free speech and self-incrimination while raising the requirement of "intent" to a level that made it difficult for prosecution to show a Communist Party member had a criminal purpose. Nonetheless the Smith Act remained and still remains on the books. Moreover, the prosecutions had been very effective in destroying the momentum of the party and burdening it with a subversive public image, which it has never totally shed.

VICTOR RABINOWITZ (1911–2007)

With the passing of Leonard Boudin, Ernest Goodman, Conrad Lynn, and William Kunstler, Victor Rabinowitz was one of the last giants of his generation on the legal left. In his memoir, *Unrepentant Leftist,* Rabinowitz tells of his long life's work, both legal and political. It is wonderfully anecdotal, well written, and covers most of the twentieth century.

Rabinowitz grew up in Brooklyn, moving several times to better and better Jewish neighborhoods as his father, Louis Rabinowitz, an immigrant from Lithuania, grew more successful. Louis Rabinowitz was an intelligent, able machinist who held several patents on hook and eye tapes. He was a radical. He supported the left wing of the Socialist Party in America. Rabinowitz's mother also came from a radical family. Her parents were close to the anarchists Emma Goldman and Alexander Berkman. Louis was a literate and cultured man who imparted his democratic values to his son. Victor went to college and law school at the University of Michigan where he was an editor of the *Michigan Law Review* and an accomplished debater.

Victor returned to New York in 1935 and joined a business law firm where he did routine corporate work. Fortunately, he was able to escape to a labor law firm. The adage in law is that your first job shapes your career. In Rabinowitz's case, it was the second. That job was with Louis Boudin, a Socialist theoretician and pioneer labor lawyer. By that time, the large organizing drives of the CIO were over, but there was still much work to be done in defense of the unions, and Victor threw himself into it with increasing skill and effectiveness.

He later formed a law firm with Leonard Boudin. Rabinowitz and Boudin (and later Michael Standard) became one of the outstanding progressive law firms in America. The Rabinowitz and Boudin firm worked first defending the labor movement (Victor was chief counsel to the union that represented the communication workers, especially the thousands in the telegraph industry).

At the end of World War II and with the passage of the anti-Communist Taft-Hartley Act, the firm went on to defend many victims of the government witch-hunt in the labor movement. They argued several cases before the Supreme Court of the United States, an extraordinary accomplishment for any lawyer, and with great skill Victor won the famous *Sabatini* case. The holding, which was later dulled (cited), made it possible for Cuba (which the firm represented after the revolution) to nationalize the United States property.

Victor was active in the movement against American participation in the Vietnam War. His partner, Leonard Boudin, was chief counsel to Dr. Spock in the famous draft card burning case and then to the Fort Jackson Eight, a case supporting civil liberties inside the military. The Socialist Workers Party (SWP) was centrally involved in the military litigation. The firm, again with Boudin as chief counsel, went on to represent the SWP in its lawsuit against the FBI and other political police. The suit resulted in the only victory among a number of similar suits. Judge Thomas Griesa issued a ruling declaring that it was legal to be a Socialist and to advocate Socialist ideas, and he granted a quarter-of-a-million-dollar judgment against the FBI and enjoined them from continuing their campaign of disruption and harassment against a legal political party.

Rabinowitz was also centrally involved in the work of the National Lawyers Guild, particularly in the '60s and early '70s, when the group, which he had helped found, was active with the New Left. He worked with people of the younger generation in passing the leadership.

Victor was the main attorney for the communication workers. He tells the story of the postwar strike for higher wages in 1947. Joe Sealy, the head of the union, was a good friend. Many other union activists and their attorneys were close personal friends as well as political associates. Those were heady days, when everything seemed possible. He says in retrospect that those were the best days of his life, days of camaraderie in the party. This is certainly a feeling that the next generation of activists can identify with. He explains how political activists, such as himself, got caught up personally and politically in the Communist Party. It was, as he so correctly explained, the only game in town. By contrast, the Socialist Workers Party was small and doctrinaire. It wasn't that he didn't know about problems in the USSR or hadn't read Trotsky. He had. His anarchist uncle had given him a copy of Trotsky's *History of the Russian Revolution*, which he compared to the "Stalinist version of events." Nor was he unaware of the Moscow purge trials, which occurred around the time he joined the party.

Rabinowitz joined the Communist Party after the Moscow trials. He was aware of them and read the transcripts, which "puzzled" him. He thought it "normal" for revolutions to be bloody, and he figured that he could still support the Soviet regime, making a parallel with Catholics who still supported their country despite the genocide against the Native Americans. He left the Communist Party in 1960 or 1961. He doesn't remember exactly when. He simply stopped attending meetings and paying his dues. He reports that the party membership declined from seventy-five thousand in 1945 to fewer than five thousand in 1958. He attributes this to Khrushchev's 1956 revelations. "His speech traumatized those of us who had weathered the domestic red hunt; the effects were felt even more severely in the highest levels of the party's structure." He goes on to say that "the result was that the party no longer performed any useful functions so far as I could see. Why? . . . Certainly its blind adherence to the Soviet Union's position on all issues and the revelations of Khrushchev's speech made its demise as a significant entity inevitable."

This of course was the position of the Socialist Workers Party from its founding in 1938. At that time, Rabinowitz writes, "The Socialist Workers Party . . . and other splinter groups seemed didactic and powerless. . . . [t]he

Communist Party was the only game in town. It led the campaign for the rights of blacks particularly in the South and in the trade unions; it was the most dynamic voice against fascism. It gave leadership to the most militant trained unions. Its agenda was my agenda."

Gil Green, a former leader of the Communist Party and its New York State chairman, who went to prison in the '50s, says simply, "I don't know where else I could have gone and got the feeling of actual participation in so many struggles."[2] Annette Rubinstein, a CP activist for more than thirty years, writes about what it was like to be part of a mass organization, feeling "that what we were doing was a necessary part of a tremendous concerted worldwide effort."[3]

Indeed, in the 1930s and 1940s it was the members of the Communist Party and their periphery that helped build the movement for black equality, organized the industrial unions, and had a vision of a multi-ethnic United States proud of its varied roots. The great irony of American radical history and the great tragedy for the American people was the CP's insistence on linking its achievements and division to a Soviet Union whose ruling party had changed into a regime of bloody repression and Byzantine cultism.

But there was another, quite different, egalitarian tradition in American radicalism that was eclipsed by the rise of the Soviet-oriented Communist Party. It was the tradition of the International Workers of the World (IWW) and the left wing of the pre–World War I Socialist Party, exemplified by Eugene V. Debs. This tradition emphasized a healthy anarchist distrust for governments, a rigorous respect for class solidarity, and a vigilant protection for freedom of speech. This tradition was represented organizationally by the International Labor Defense (ILD).

The founding principles and activities of the International Labor Defense (ILD) provide us with an example worth emulating. James P. Cannon of

[2] Michael E. Brown, Randy Martin, Frank Rosengarten and George Snedeker, eds., *New Studies in the Politics and Culture of U.S. Communism* (New York: Monthly Review Press, 1993).

[3] Ibid.

Rosedale, Kansas was the founder of the ILD. Prior to World War I, Cannon was active in the IWW and worked with the legendary Vincent St. John and William "Big Bill" Haywood. In 1919, after the success of the Russian revolution, Cannon was a founder and principal leader of the new Communist Party of the United States of America. In 1925, he spent most of the year in Moscow working with other revolutionaries from around the world who constituted the Communist International. Cannon met extensively with Haywood, then living in political exile. They agreed on the need for a defense organization in America that would provide political, legal, and material support for those who they termed "class-war prisoners." They understood that legal argument alone, while important, was insufficient and that a movement in the streets outside of the legal process, which sought to win public opinion, was required if victims of capitalist injustice were to be adequately defended. They called this "mass defense."

The ILD was non-sectarian and supported victims from various political tendencies, the most famous being the two Italian immigrant anarchists Sacco and Vanzetti. Cannon was removed from the leadership of the ILD when he was expelled from the Communist Party in 1928 as an early opponent of the Stalinist degeneration in the Soviet Union. Under his leadership the ILD believed in and acted upon the old IWW principle, "an injury to one is an injury to all." Added to this principle of solidarity was the idea of universality. Fred Halstead, a leader of the anti-Vietnam war movement and himself the son of an IWW member stated it simply: "We are for civil liberties here and everywhere, now and after the revolution." The principles of solidarity, non-sectarianism, and internationalism were lost in the mire of the Stalinized Communist Party, but they will be reasserted in the future, for they indeed provide the movement with the guidelines for success.

The CP's destruction as a political force came not so much from its own hand as by massive governmental repression, a repression made all the more easy by linking the CP to the "evil" Soviet Union. Thus did Socialism lose its moral authority and fall into the crisis from which it is only now emerging.

But it was Stalinism that died, not Socialism. The *Communist Manifesto* is only one hundred fifty years old. Nowhere has Socialism as a state been introduced into a developed capitalist society as the authors of the *Manifesto* envisioned. Capitalism, on the other hand, has developed over the last six hundred years from its beginnings in Venice and the Hanseatic cities to its present day global manifestation.

Those who take the long view of history will acknowledge the contributions of Victor Rabinowitz and his generation of comrades in their contradictory contest and learn from their experiences.

LEONARD BOUDIN (1912–1989)

Leonard Boudin was the great leftist constitutional defense lawyer of his time. His career spanned five decades beginning in the 1930s.

Paul Robeson, the eminent African American actor and singer who, blacklisted for his Communist politics, declared he would "not retreat one thousandth part of an inch"; Julian Bond, who co-founded the Student Nonviolent Coordinating Committee and later became a Georgia state senator; Dr. Benjamin Spock, the best-selling public health author accused of corrupting the '60s youth; Daniel Ellsberg, whose leaking of the Pentagon Papers blew the lid on the Vietnam War; Jimmy Hoffa, the Teamsters union boss—Boudin defended all these people, and more.

He won a crucial Supreme Court decision in 1958 (*Kent v. Dulles*) that passports cannot be withheld by the State Department for political reasons. He was the legal representative of Cuba's interests in America from the early days of the Cuban revolution. He also represented the Central Bank of Iran when assets of the Iranian government were seized by the United States.

He litigated and won three cases for the Socialist Workers Party (SWP) and its youth affiliate, the Young Socialist Alliance (YSA), which protected Socialists' right to exist, to associate, to speak, and to organize. These rights, hard-won, remain crucially important today.

The first of these victories was in Indiana. Three Socialist students at the University of Indiana, all members of the YSA, were indicted for seeking to overthrow the State of Indiana under the Indiana Communist Act. The prosecutor declared, "We only want to stamp out Communism and what it stands for before it gets a foothold here." The students had been active in organizing a rally in support of the Cuban revolution and then in bringing a speaker on the campus who defended the right of black people to armed self-defense against racist violence that was sweeping the South in response to the civil rights movement.

Boudin was chief counsel of the Emergency Civil Liberties Committee, which took the case and agreed to pay for it. The Bloomington Defense Committee was formed to reach out to everyone who wanted to oppose the witch hunt. To support the committee required agreement that the YSA had a right to exist and that it had a right to free speech and assembly. It got wide support from people and organizations who agreed with these democratic principles.

The case was won in the lower court, reversed in the Indiana Supreme Court, and was ultimately struck down as unconstitutional by federal court. It set the precedent that such laws in other states were also unconstitutional. "The effective defense campaign did more than help push back the witch hunt. The defendants were able to turn the tables on the prosecutors and the cops by exposing their contempt for democratic rights and the Constitution," wrote Barry Sheppard, the national secretary of the YSA at the time.

Leonard Boudin litigated the case *Socialist Workers Party v. Attorney General* as chief counsel for the SWP in the fifteen-year litigation that ended in a historic victory in 1986. The case is extraordinarily important today. *The Nation* magazine appreciated the significance of the litigation and wrote that "for the first time the FBI's disruptions, surreptitious entries and use of informers have been found unconstitutional. All in all, it amounted to a domestic contra-operation against a lawful and peaceful political organization, for no reason other than its ideological orientation."

Boudin wrote that "this lawsuit represented the first wholesale attack upon the entire hierarchy of so-called intelligence agencies that had attempted to infiltrate and destroy a lawful political party." Further, "for the first time a court has really examined the FBI's intrusions into the political system of our nation and, in unmistakable language, has condemned the FBI activity as patently unconstitutional and without statutory or regulatory authority. The decision stands as a vindication of the First and Fourth Amendment rights not only of the Socialist Workers Party but of all political organizations and activists in the country to be free of government spying and harassment."

I met Leonard almost fifty years ago during the height of the anti-war movement on an army base near Columbia, South Carolina—Fort Jackson. He was there to represent the Fort Jackson Nine and I was there to help.

The nine men, mostly black and Puerto Rican, had just been placed in the stockade for organizing an anti-war rally of two hundred fifty men in uniform on the base. The Pentagon had flipped out.

I had just gotten out of law school and was with a Lawyers Guild firm in Detroit. Leonard was a fifty-seven-year-old veteran of the good fight and deeply admired for his legal skill. He was too utterly charming and gentle and witty and wonderful to be around. We met in town and I drove him out to the base.

Fort Jackson's main street was an extension of a main street in Columbia, a city that has twice won the All-American City award. You could drive about it freely. The base had a grotesque resemblance to a small American town. There were railroad tracks, bus stops, taxis, grocery stores, and women with children in tow. *The Green Berets* was playing at the base theater.

A platoon of men taking bayonet practice was marched past our car. "What are you here to do?" the sergeant yelled. "To kill!" "How?" "Without mercy!"

"I used to be for dismantling all foreign bases," said Leonard, "but now I think I'm for dismantling all domestic ones as well."

The men in the stockade had organized, with Leonard's advice, a group they named GIs United Against the War in Vietnam. To join you had to agree with two things: that ordinary GIs had the same rights as other citizens to make their opinions known to their elected representatives, and that there were a lot of racist practices in the army.

How did a New York lawyer come to represent GIs in South Carolina? Leonard was counsel to the GI Civil Liberties Defense Committee (GICLDC). Bertrand Russell was the group's honorary chairman and the committee had wide support throughout the peace movement. But it was initiated and staffed by members of the Socialist Workers Party and its youth affiliate, the Young Socialist Alliance. There was a sectarian aversion toward these two groups in the Guild and in and around the Communist Party. This didn't faze Leonard.

He understood the potential of organizing GIs around First Amendment rights to speak out and act out against the war. After all, who had more at stake? And who was in a more strategic position to end the war than the GIs themselves? Leonard met with leaders of the GICLDC. They agreed to counsel GIs to do everything legal that the army commanded. But—and this was the genius of the tactic—they projected a group that would petition their congressmen, put out newspapers and leaflets, and march and urge others to march in the giant anti-war demonstrations of the time.

The men were, in this conception, citizen-soldiers, whose First Amendment rights couldn't be abridged simply because they had been drafted or enlisted in the army.

Leonard was miles ahead of most of the anti-war movement on this. Where much of the movement was urging draft resistance and disdained the ordinary "killer" GI, Leonard understood precisely where power lay and how to organize it. And that's how he got to South Carolina representing GIs forty years his junior who were in and around a political tendency he by no means agreed with.

I asked him once if he was a Socialist. He demurred, smiling, and said no but that a lot of the most interesting people around him were. I didn't believe him. Later a friend told me she saw him reading a book about the history of the First International. A pretty esoteric interest for someone who wasn't a Socialist.

I also asked him how he came to set his legal fees. We were eating in a diner. He thought about it for a second and answered, "I think of what a fair fee would be, look the client straight in the eye, double it, and say it." Of course, he wasn't in it for the money, but I always remembered that advice. Leonard knew how to run a movement practice without running it into the ground.

What happened to the Fort Jackson Nine? First it was disclosed that one of the nine was a military police informer. That caused a big stink—denial of the right to counsel—and got lots more publicity, even the front page of the *New York Times*.

So it became the Fort Jackson Eight. Free the Fort Jackson Eight rallies were held on campuses and in cities around the country. Publicity snowballed. Even *Playboy* had an article about the plight of the citizen-soldier who obeyed orders but reserved the right to make his opinion known.

The trial of the Eight began. Leonard took sick—even then he had heart problems—and Guild attorney David Rein came down from D.C. to take on the army. Meanwhile, the prosecution began to be directed from the Pentagon.

They couldn't logically refute the formulation of citizen-soldier. Anti-war feeling mounted in the country. A message was smuggled out of the stockade from the Eight and read to a mass rally in Atlanta. Hundreds of thousands rallied around the country against the war. GIs United started in North Carolina and their literature was being passed around in Vietnam.

The cover story by muckraker journalist Robert Sherrill, titled "Military Music Is to Music as Military Justice Is to Justice," appeared in the Sunday *New York Times* magazine section. And finally, the Pentagon folded.

They dropped the charges against the remaining prisoners and let them out of the army. Then the Pentagon, in one of the most significant victories of the anti-war movement, passed a new set of regulations allowing GIs to possess anti-war literature and to march in anti-war demonstrations.

It was the beginning of the end of American intervention into the Vietnamese revolution. And Leonard Boudin was there at the start.

Originally published in Michael Steven Smith, Lawyers You'll Like: Putting Human Rights First *(Union City, N.J.: Smyrna Press, 1999).*

AFTERWORD

"Justice is a constant struggle" is the motto of the National Lawyers Guild, this nation's oldest human rights bar association. It could have served as the title of this wonderfully informative, insightful, and inspiring book. After all, so many of the struggles documented in the book have been ongoing, or are repeating themselves today.

The interviews describing the work of lawyers who defended the heroic civil rights movement in the South in the '60s has its modern-day expression in the work today of lawyers defending the Black Lives Matter movement, as it fights back against the epidemic of police murders of young black people; and, as I write this afterword, Lawyers Guild attorneys are in Mexico, near the U.S. border, assisting Latin American immigrants who've marched hundreds of miles to the Mexican–U.S. border, in the hopes of securing political asylum in America. Attorneys are essential to this effort, given the extreme xenophobia that has America in its grip; a form of racism no less insidious than the anti-black racism in the South in the '60s . . . or today.

In the late '60s and early '70s, the "peoples' lawyers" were also defending anti-Vietnam War protesters: defending their right to march in the streets, defending them when indicted for refusing induction, and defending them when, as members of the armed services, they resisted unlawful military commands. The same is true again today, this time on behalf of those protesting the U.S. wars in Iraq and Afghanistan, or in the streets demanding that the United States stop funding Israel's murderous attacks in Gaza.

This book recounts the illegal spying by the government in the '60s and '70s through its COINTELPRO operation, whereby the FBI spied on anti-war, civil rights, and women's rights groups. Today, the FBI infiltrates Islamic mosques in an effort to seduce members into spying on fellow members who may have strident anti-American political views. Also, today, in cities all across America, programs are in place whereby residents are encouraged to report "suspicious activities" to the police; and a file is secretly opened on the person engaged in the allegedly "suspicious activity," and becomes a part of a database full of similar files, all kept in secret by the government with the subjects of the files never the wiser nor, of course, given a chance to refute the information in their file. And, of course, plain "old fashioned" government spying on political groups and activists, a la COINTELPRO-styled undercover work, never really ceased to operate.

The chapter containing the interview with attorney Rhonda Copelon and her work under the Alien Tort Act in the *Filártiga* case, is reminiscent of the case of *Dogan v. Barak*, argued in May 2018. *Dogan* is a case seeking redress for the torture and murder of an American citizen while aboard one of the ships seeking to bring humanitarian aid to Gaza. And this current case demonstrates the difficult and "constant struggle" to successfully sue a foreign national in a U.S. court of law, given this nation's desire to protect its allies from such lawsuits, even when its allies, as Israel has done in the *Dogan* case, commit heinous crimes against one of America's citizens.

Also illustrative of the constancy of the struggle for justice is the ongoing fight for the rights of workers in capitalist America. From the Flint sit-down strike of 1937, to the massive walk-outs and protests by America's teachers today, the demands are essentially the same: decent working conditions. A fair wage.

The battles around Wounded Knee find their modern counterpart in today's battles at Standing Rock and the effort to stop an oil pipeline crossing through sacred native Indian land in the Dakotas.

Today, with trade unions weakened to the point where only 10–11 percent of the labor force is unionized; where the Socialist groups that provided leadership in past for progressive struggles have seen a similar reduction in membership; and at a time when Corporate America is more completely in control of the electoral process than at any prior point in U.S. history; the need for Socialists and progressives and, yes, liberals, to find a way to at least "unite in action," if not structurally, is greater than ever.

And the failure of these forces to thus far find that unity in action is particularly tragic given the opening created by the surprisingly strong showing by Bernie Sanders in the 2016 presidential election. Sanders self-identified as a Socialist, at least a "Democratic Socialist." And it's now clear that the idea of Socialism, like the word itself, is no longer a word of derision, but a word and a system of governance enjoying surprisingly wide support among the people of America. In fact, polls show most young people think a Socialist country is preferable to a capitalist one.

Also, the demonstrated opposition to the Trump regime is monumental. When one considers the massive protests that have taken place at the time of his inauguration and on its anniversary, as well as the rallies by the young for gun control in over eight hundred towns on a single day, it is the case that perhaps more Americans, on a given day, have been in the streets demanding social and economic justice than at any other time in U.S. history.

In this context, a failure of the left to find a way to unite to fight for changes supported by a majority of Americans is tragic. Single-payer health coverage; a higher tax rate for the rich; an increase in welfare benefits for the less well-off; and support for allowing undocumented immigrants to stay in America are all supported by a majority of the American people. But they can only be realized by a united movement fighting for their realization.

It's the only way we've won such battles in the past. Think of the long struggle for a woman's right to an abortion. It ended when the same all-male Supreme Court that had previously denied such a right changed its mind and issued its ruling in *Roe v. Wade*. That "change of mind" didn't come about simply because those nine men woke up one morning and said to themselves, "Jesus, have we been a bunch of sexists! Of course a woman has the right to choose!"

No, their minds were changed as a consequence of hundreds of thousands of women and men refusing to stop marching in the streets and sitting-in in legislator's offices and getting arrested, demanding the right to choose.

In the '30s and '40s, it wasn't the goodwill of the factory owners that produced unions and collective bargaining, or laws against child labor. It was the union movement marching and striking and sitting-in and facing down the Pinkertons that brought about unions and advanced workers' rights.

The same was true with respect to the victories of the civil rights movement and the gay rights movement. For sure, a court or some legislature ultimately rendered a ruling or passed a piece of legislation favoring civil rights and gay rights—but only after, and because, a powerful movement in the streets had demanded no less. Indeed, had demanded more.

Perhaps the most dramatic and convincing proof of a mass movement's power was demonstrated by the movement against the U.S. War in Vietnam. That war was ended under Republican presidents, Nixon and Ford. No doubt, the victories on the battlefield by the Viet Cong were critical. But the war ended when it did primarily because of a massive and broad-based movement of Americans, in the streets, who finally made it impossible for any U.S. administration to continue the war, be it a Republican or Democratic administration.

And so the central lesson of the great struggles of the past, and those of the present, documented so clearly in this book, is that what's most important is not who is sitting in the White House or the Congress, or in state legislative halls, but who is marching in the streets of America.

This is why the need for unity among today's progressive movements is so critical, so in need of being realized. In this regard, Michael Smith, the author of this book, along with myself and another comrade, Ronald Reosti, have tried over the past few years to get those groups who identify as "Socialist" to at least unite in action. (And so far none have denied its need.) What we've proposed is the creation of a Socialist "network." Such a network would leave all groups and Socialist parties that join it free to carry on with their own work, asking only that once or twice a year they would unite around a mutually agreed common campaign, for example to demand a single-payer health care system. Such a network could also work in harmony or coalition with labor groups and liberal groups of all stripes, thus presenting a much more powerful adversary than presently exists to the entrenched capitalist interests opposing such a health care system. The struggle for this much-needed unity will continue.

Finally, it is my hope that the political activists who read this book, be they organizers or attorneys, will not only be inspired by the extraordinary work of those who came before them, but will also leave determined to forge the powerful political unity that today's battles require if victory is to be won. And, of course, what is the history of such battles if not that such victories *can* be won? Indeed, with history itself on our side, our day, that day of social, economic, and political justice that those interviewed in this book fought for so heroically, can and must be won!

Jim Lafferty

APPENDIX: LAW IN A SOCIALIST SOCIETY

What would law be like if we didn't have capitalism in America, if we replaced it and were able to live in a genuinely Socialist society? Imagine a society of ecological sanity, material abundance, and social equality; a society where social relations are premised on human solidarity, not capitalist exploitation and human competition; where people are not set against each other; where production for profit, driven by private greed and accumulation of capital, has given way to production for public use.

To envision what the law would become, we need to understand where it came from. Law is not a fixed system but an evolving one, bound up with changing social conditions. The law we have now—contracts, property, corporate, trusts and estates, domestic relations, torts (injuries)—is based on the ownership of private property (corporations and banks, not toothbrushes). But it wasn't always that way.

A thousand years ago, Europe was a feudal society with different social conditions and different laws. Feudal society was static. Land ownership was frozen in relatively wealthy, propertied families. Trade and commerce were confined to luxury goods for the rich. Charging of interest on loans was forbidden, thereby inhibiting commerce and banking. Life centered on isolated villages and the large manor houses of the nobility. Most people were serfs, semi-slaves bound for life to an aristocratic ruler. How did this change into what we have now?

The modern bourgeoisie, or ruling class, or the "1 percent" as the Occupy movement famously describes them, started off as part of the 99 percent. They began their long march to power as humble merchants in medieval Europe. They were the early capitalists in what was then a feudal society. The law they created and refined over the years is the law we live under today. (Legal scholars Michael Tigar and Madeleine R. Levy pioneered the study of the history of the law, which they developed in their book *Law and the Rise of Capitalism.*)

These bourgeois revolutionaries brought about a newly dominant legal ideology based upon a different system of social relations. They sought old legal forms—mainly Roman—and invested them with a new commercial content. They also used canon (church) law, royal law, feudal law, and "natural law" (common sense) to construct a socially protected system of commerce as well as to promote, and thereby profit more from, advances in technology.

In pursuit of their material interests, the bourgeoisie established the freedom of contract, with the ability to sell land and to lend and borrow money with interest. They devised laws to regulate all this, courts to adjudicate disputes, and a central power to enforce their judgments. These were all preconditions for the growth of modern society. In large measure, the medieval bourgeoisie and their lawyers prepared the way for today's possibility of abundance.

Significant legal change is the product of conflict between social classes seeking to turn the institutions of social control to their own purposes and to impose and maintain a specific system of socioeconomic relations. The transformation from the legal system in feudal times took some eight hundred years. The rising bourgeoisie couldn't buy property freely in a real-estate market or associate politically or economically. They were social outcasts whose profit-taking was thought to be dishonorable, a form of usury that put their souls in jeopardy. Called *pies poudreuse,* or dusty feet, they peddled their goods from market to town to fair.

But this disreputable lot first accommodated to, then openly confronted, and finally overthrew the legal ideology of feudalism. They subordinated and sacrificed all of feudalism's ties of personal fealty and hierarchy to capitalism's bonds of cash and contract. The French Enlightenment philosopher Denis Diderot described the mode of their progress: "The strange god settles himself humbly on the altar beside the god of the country. Little by little he establishes himself firmly. Then one fine morning he gives his neighbor a shove with his elbow and crash!—the idol lies upon the ground."

After accumulating for centuries in the feudal formations, capitalist law cataclysmically replaced feudal law in the English and French revolutions of the seventeenth and eighteenth centuries. This historical precedent can help us understand how the law will change again to reflect different property relations in the transition to Socialism.

Karl Marx and Friedrich Engels put forward what subsequently became known as the commodity theory of law. Marx identified the material premises of our prevailing legal relations and set them forth in his book, *Capital*. The legal system, swollen with codes, courts, law schools, law-making bodies, publications, and prisons, is based on transactions bound up with the production of articles for exchange, money, and the rights of private property. Under capitalism's system of generalized commodity production, individuals became legal subjects having rights, especially contractual rights, to buy and sell commodities—including the power of labor, which itself is a commodity. The buyer and the seller exchange equivalents, things that are equal in value. Law regulates this exchange, and the state enforces the law.

An equal standard is applied. No allowance is made for the natural inequality of individual talent. As Marx wrote, "A given amount of labor in one form is exchanged for an equal amount of labor in another form." However, he concluded, that bourgeois right, embedded in market relations, is superficial and formal. The social and economic inequalities between the classes restrict and negate it.

In this system, the ruling minority of the rich monopolizes the means of production, while the working people are dispossessed. In order to live, they must sell their labor power to a boss at the prevailing wage rates. This transaction, which conforms to the rules of the market and the legal code, appears fair to both sides. But it really masks a relation of inequality, because workers produce more value in the process of production than they are paid for. That is the source of their exploitation. Bourgeois law justifies this unjust state of affairs.

Since commodity relations will continue to persist in the United States as we make the transition from capitalism to Socialism, our laws will continue to reflect bourgeois norms, however mitigated, because of unavoidable inequalities. The state and the law it upholds will eventually become unnecessary when there is an abundance of goods and the individual exchange of equivalents through the market becomes unnecessary. Even now, in our capitalist society, we see a glimpse of the future in employee stock-ownership programs, the forty-eight thousand cooperatives that market 30 percent of all farm produce, and in publicly owned banks, life-insurance companies, electric and water companies, hospitals, cable TV stations, and Internet providers.

In a rationally, democratically organized society that has done away with capitalist private property, which is used only to produce for profit and not for human needs, that day will come fairly soon. Legal institutions as we know them, and the juridical element in social relations, must gradually disappear as commodity relations die out.

The rule will become "from each according to their ability, to each according to their need." There will be no need for law as we know it. Human relations will become regulated more by custom, as they once were before the advent of class society.

Law in America is sold as an impartial force for justice and equality. Its origins are shrouded in mystery and invested with the sanction of tradition. Most people have trouble buying this proposition, as indicated by the public-opinion polls that find lawyers to be the second-most unpopular group of professionals in the country, just behind politicians. The fraudulence of the formal equality of rights and the apparent neutrality of judges was brilliantly pierced by Anatole France's oft-quoted remark that the law in all its majesty forbids all persons, whether rich or poor, from sleeping under bridges.

With Socialism in America, the people will own the bridges, and they'll sleep peacefully and contentedly with a roof over their heads knowing that they have created a society in which the law won't work against them and, in the words of the great *Communist Manifesto*, "where the free development of each is the condition of the free development of all."

Originally published as Michael Steven Smith, "Law in a Socialist USA," in Frances Goldin et al., eds., Imagine Living in a Socialist USA *(New York: Harper Perennial, 2014), 53–57.*

ACKNOWLEDGMENTS

I would like to thank my comrade and wife of forty-four years, Debby Ginsburg Smith, for her help in shaping the book. Thank you as well to my friends and comrades Heidi Boghosian and Jim Lafferty for their foreword and afterword. Thanks also to Dalia Hashad, who was an initial co-host of *Law and Disorder Radio* when we started out. My appreciation to our producer Geoff Brady, who so expertly recorded these interviews. I appreciate as well my cousin Fania Smith Cornelius and her husband, David Cornelius, for editing the interviews. My publisher and friend, Colin Robinson, is a dream to work with. Thank you to his team of Jamie Stern-Weiner and Emma Ingrisani for their intelligent editing. OR Books is a wonderful, innovative political publishing company and it is an honor to be published by them.

I would also like to acknowledge the Puffin Foundation, whose financial support to *Law and Disorder Radio* made a number of these interviews possible.

INDEX

INDEX

ABOUT THE AUTHOR

Michael Steven Smith was born in Chicago in 1942 and grew up in the lakeside village of Fox Point, north of Milwaukee, Wisconsin. He attended the University of Wisconsin, where he was a student of the great social historian Harvey Goldberg.

Smith graduated from the university in 1964 and from its law school in 1967. He practiced public service law in Detroit, working in the inner city with Community Legal Counsel and then Neighborhood Legal Services.

He was a founding member of the Detroit movement law firm Lafferty, Reosti, Jabara, Papahkian, James, Stickgold, Smith, and Soble, about which the Detroit Police Department Red Squad wrote that "[t]here is hardly an underground newspaper, Black liberation, or left-wing group of any kind in Detroit that at one time or another was not represented by the law firm."

After moving to New York City, he worked at Harlem Legal Services before establishing Seafarers Legal Services, where he represented indigent merchant mariners. He later went on to represent seriously injured people in lawsuits against insurance companies.

Smith has served on the boards of the Center for Constitutional Rights, the Left Forum, the Brecht Forum, and the New York City chapter of the National

Lawyers Guild. He has testified on Palestinian human rights before committees of the U.S. Congress and United Nations.

Smith has written the memoir *Notebook of a Sixties Lawyer.* With Michael Ratner, he wrote *How the CIA Killed Che*, and with Frances Goldin and Deborah Smith he co-edited the book *Imagine: Living in a Socialist USA*.

With Michael Ratner, Heidi Boghosian, and Dalia Hashad, he founded the nationally broadcast radio show *Law and Disorder,* which has been on the air since 2004.